Pennsylvania Real Estate Test

Pennsylvania Real Estate License Exam: Best Test Prep Book to Help You Get Your License!

The Ultimate Workbook: Salesperson and Broker Exam-Passing Strategies

By: Blueocean Experts
Table of Content

1. Introduction………………………………………………………………….3
2. Understanding the Pennsylvania Real Estate Market……...............……5
3. Eligibility Criteria………………………………………………………….8
4. Application Process………………………………………………………13
5. Exam Format………………………………………………………………18
6. Property Ownership and Land Use Controls………………………...22
   - Mock Exam Property Ownership and Land Use Controls…………26
7. Laws of Agency and Fiduciary Duties…………………………………44
   - Mock Exam Laws of Agency and Fiduciary Duties………………...49
8. Property Valuation and Financial Analysis……………………..……67
   - Mock Exam Property Valuation and Financial Analysis……………71
9. Financing……………………………………………………………………88
   - Mock Exam Financing…………………………………………………93
10. Transfer of Property……………………………………………...……110
    - Mock Exam Transfer of Property……………………………………114
11. Practice of Real Estate and Disclosures……………………………131
    - Mock Exam Practice of Real Estate and Disclosures………………136
12. Contracts……………………………………………………………...…153
    - Mock Exam Contracts………………………………………………157
13. Real Estate Calculations………………………………………………175
    - Mock Exam Real Estate Calculations………………………………180
14. Specialty Areas…………………………………………………………197
    - Mock Exam Specialty Areas…………………………………………202
15. Ethics and Legal Considerations……………………………………219
    - Mock Exam Ethics and Legal Considerations……………………...222
16. Day of the Exam………………………………………………………240
17. After the Exam: Next Steps…………………………………………244
18. Career Development…………………………………………………248
19. Conclusion…………………………………………………………...…253

Introduction

Dear Aspiring Real Estate Professional,

Congratulations on taking the first step toward a rewarding career in real estate! By picking up this book, "Pennsylvania Real Estate License Exam: Best Test Prep Book to Help You Get Your License!", you're not just investing in a study guide—you're investing in your future. The decision to pursue a career in real estate is a life-changing one, and this book aims to be your steadfast companion on this exciting journey.

Why Pennsylvania? The Keystone of Opportunities

Pennsylvania, often referred to as the Keystone State, is a state of diverse opportunities in the real estate market. From the bustling, historic streets of Philadelphia to the serene, picturesque landscapes of the Pocono Mountains, Pennsylvania offers a unique blend of urban and rural living. Whether you're interested in residential, commercial, or industrial real estate, Pennsylvania provides a fertile ground for a thriving career. The state's rich history and diverse geography make it a hotspot for real estate activities, offering something for everyone.

What This Book Offers: Your Comprehensive Guide

This book is meticulously designed to be a comprehensive guide that helps you navigate the complexities of the Pennsylvania real estate license exam. But it's not just about passing the test; it's about equipping you with the tools you need to be successful in your career long after the exam is over. We'll cover everything from the foundational knowledge of real estate principles to the specific laws and regulations that govern the industry in Pennsylvania.

Structure of the Book: A Step-by-Step Guide

The book is organized into several key sections, each designed to build upon the last. We'll start with an in-depth overview of the Pennsylvania real estate market, followed by chapters on eligibility criteria, the application process, and the exam format. We'll delve into specific topics like contracts, property valuation, ethics, and much more. Each chapter concludes with a set of meticulously crafted practice questions to test your understanding of the material and prepare you for the exam.

Mock Exams for Real Success: Your Secret Weapon

One of the standout features of this book is the inclusion of mock exams. These are designed to simulate the actual exam experience closely. The questions are crafted based on the most current Pennsylvania real estate laws and market trends, ensuring that you're as prepared as possible for the real thing. These mock exams are your secret weapon for success, offering you the closest experience to the actual exam.

Beyond the Exam: Building a Lasting Career

But this book is more than just a test prep guide. The latter sections focus on what comes after you've passed your exam—how to launch your career, continue your education, and adhere to ethical standards. We'll also explore career development strategies to help you decide which path within real estate is the best fit for you. We'll guide you through networking, choosing a brokerage, and even how to market yourself effectively.

Your Journey Starts Now: Let's Build Your Future Together

As you turn the pages of this book, you're not just learning; you're taking actionable steps toward a fulfilling and potentially lucrative career. We're thrilled to be part of your journey and are committed to providing you with the most comprehensive, up-to-date information possible.

Thank you for choosing "Pennsylvania Real Estate License Exam: Best Test Prep Book to Help You Get Your License!" as your guide. Here's to your future success in the Pennsylvania real estate industry!

Understanding the Pennsylvania Real Estate Market

The real estate market in Pennsylvania is a microcosm of the larger economic, social, and cultural trends that shape the state. Understanding this market requires a multi-faceted approach, considering everything from historical landmarks to emerging tech hubs. This chapter aims to offer an in-depth analysis of the Pennsylvania real estate market, dissecting its complexities and providing actionable insights for prospective buyers, sellers, and investors.

- Historical Context

Pennsylvania's history is deeply intertwined with the formation and growth of the United States. Cities like Philadelphia are not just historical landmarks but also vibrant real estate markets. The state's history has led to a unique blend of architectural styles, from colonial and Victorian homes to modern condos and office spaces. This rich historical tapestry adds layers of complexity to the real estate market, making it essential for buyers and sellers to understand the historical significance of the areas they are interested in.

- Historical Preservation

The state has numerous historical districts where property sales and modifications are subject to regulations to preserve the area's historical character. This can impact property values and should be a consideration for any potential investment.

- Market Segmentation

Urban Markets

Philadelphia: Beyond its historical significance, Philadelphia is a burgeoning tech hub, a cultural melting pot, and a city of neighborhoods, each with its unique real estate micro-market. Areas like Northern Liberties have seen an influx of young professionals, driving up property values and spurring commercial development.

Pittsburgh: Once an industrial giant, Pittsburgh has reinvented itself as a center for healthcare, education, and technology. Neighborhoods like Lawrenceville offer a mix of residential and commercial opportunities, attracting a diverse demographic.

Suburban Markets

The suburbs offer a different lifestyle, marked by residential communities, shopping centers, and schools. Towns like King of Prussia are experiencing growth due to their proximity to job markets in Philadelphia and a surge in new developments.

Rural Markets

The rural real estate market is often overlooked but offers unique investment opportunities. From farmlands in Lancaster County to vacation homes in the Pocono Mountains, rural properties can offer significant returns on investment.

- Economic Factors

Job Market

The job market in Pennsylvania is diverse, with significant contributions from the healthcare, education, and tech industries. Cities with robust job markets like Philadelphia and Pittsburgh have seen a corresponding rise in property values and rental rates.

Cost of Living

Pennsylvania offers a relatively affordable cost of living compared to its neighboring states, making it an attractive option for first-time homebuyers and investors alike.

- Market Trends

Gentrification

Areas around major cities are experiencing gentrification, leading to rising property values but also posing challenges like displacement of long-term residents.

Sustainability

The demand for sustainable living is on the rise, with more buyers looking for energy-efficient homes and communities with green spaces.

Investment Opportunities

With a diverse range of properties, from multi-family units to commercial spaces, Pennsylvania offers a plethora of investment opportunities. Understanding the tax implications, zoning laws, and other regulatory factors is crucial for prospective investors.

- Conclusion

Understanding the Pennsylvania real estate market is a complex but rewarding endeavor. With its rich history, diverse economic landscape, and a wide range of property types, the state offers something for everyone. Whether you're a first-time homebuyer, a seasoned investor, or someone looking to relocate, understanding the intricacies of this market will serve you well in making informed decisions.

Eligibility Criteria

The path to becoming a real estate agent in Pennsylvania is paved with various steps, each requiring careful attention to detail. One of the most crucial steps is understanding the eligibility criteria. This chapter aims to serve as a comprehensive guide, breaking down each requirement in detail, from age and educational prerequisites to background checks and financial stability.

- Age Requirements

Minimum Age

The first and foremost requirement for becoming a real estate agent in Pennsylvania is age. You must be at least 18 years old to apply for a real estate license. This age requirement is consistent across many states and is a non-negotiable factor.

Age Verification

Verifying your age is a straightforward process but an essential one. You will need to provide a government-issued identification, such as a driver's license or a passport, during the application process. Make sure your identification is current and valid to avoid any complications.

- Educational Requirements

Pre-License Education

Before you can even think about taking the real estate license exam, you must complete a mandatory 75 hours of pre-license education from a school approved by the Pennsylvania Real Estate Commission. This education is divided into two main courses:

1. Real Estate Fundamentals (30 hours): This course provides a foundational understanding of real estate principles, including property types, ownership forms, and basic contract law. It's the bedrock upon which your real estate knowledge will be built.

2. Real Estate Practice (45 hours): This course is more hands-on, focusing on the day-to-day operations of a real estate agent. Topics include listing properties, conducting valuations, and understanding ethical considerations.

Proof of Education

Upon completion of these courses, you will receive a certificate or transcript, which you must submit as part of your application. Make sure to keep copies for your records as well.

Continuing Education

Once you're licensed, the learning doesn't stop. Pennsylvania requires real estate agents to complete 14 hours of continuing education every two years to renew their license. This ensures that agents stay up-to-date with the latest industry trends and legal changes.

- Background Checks

Criminal History

A criminal background check is mandatory for all applicants. While having a criminal record doesn't automatically disqualify you, certain offenses, particularly those related to fraud or financial crimes, could make it difficult to obtain a license.

Fingerprinting

The background check process includes fingerprinting, which is usually conducted by the Pennsylvania State Police or an authorized agency. This is an additional layer of verification to ensure the safety and integrity of the real estate profession.

Disclosure Requirements

Transparency is key when applying for a real estate license. You must disclose any criminal history or ongoing legal issues. Failure to do so can result in immediate disqualification or future revocation of your license.

- Financial Stability

Credit Score Considerations

While Pennsylvania doesn't have a strict credit score requirement, your financial history will be scrutinized. A poor credit score could raise questions about your financial responsibility, which is a key aspect of being a real estate agent.

Bankruptcy and Financial History

Having a bankruptcy in your past won't automatically disqualify you, but it will require you to provide additional documentation and possibly go through a review process. The commission may ask for proof that you have resolved the issues that led to bankruptcy and are now financially stable.

- Examination Requirements

The Pennsylvania Real Estate Salesperson Exam

This is the final hurdle in your journey to becoming a licensed real estate agent. The exam is divided into two parts: the national portion, which covers general real estate principles, and the state-specific portion, which focuses on laws and regulations unique to Pennsylvania.

Exam Fees

The cost of taking the exam is approximately $49, and this fee is non-refundable. Make sure to review the payment methods accepted by your chosen testing center.

Exam Retakes

If you don't pass the exam on your first try, don't worry. You can retake it, but you'll need to wait for a specified period and pay the exam fee again.

- Application Process

Online vs. Paper Applications

Pennsylvania offers the convenience of both online and paper applications. However, online applications are generally processed faster and are becoming the more popular option.

Application Fees

The application fee for a real estate salesperson license in Pennsylvania is around $107. This fee is non-refundable and must be submitted along with your application.

License Issuance

Once you've met all the requirements and passed the exam, you'll receive your license. The Pennsylvania Real Estate Commission usually takes 4-6 weeks to process and mail out licenses.

- Special Cases

Reciprocity Agreements

Pennsylvania has reciprocity agreements with several states. This means that if you're already a licensed real estate agent in a state with which Pennsylvania has an agreement, you can become licensed in Pennsylvania without taking the state exam. However, you'll still need to meet all other eligibility criteria.

Military Personnel and Spouses

If you're in the military or married to someone who is, you may be eligible for certain accommodations, such as fee waivers or expedited application processes.

- Conclusion

Understanding the eligibility criteria is the first step in your journey to becoming a real estate agent in Pennsylvania. This chapter has aimed to provide a detailed guide to help you navigate these requirements. From age and education to background checks and financial stability, we've covered each aspect to set you on the path to a successful career in real estate.

Application Process

The application process for obtaining a real estate license in Pennsylvania is a multi-step journey that requires careful planning, attention to detail, and a thorough understanding of the state's specific requirements. This chapter aims to serve as a comprehensive guide to help you navigate this complex process, from initial preparations to the final submission of your application.

- Preparing for the Application

Documentation

Before you start the application process, gather all the necessary documents. This includes:

- *Proof of Age:* A government-issued ID, such as a driver's license or passport.
- *Educational Certificates:* Transcripts or certificates from your pre-license education courses.
- *Background Check:* A copy of your criminal background check and fingerprinting results.
- *Financial Documents:* While not mandatory, having your financial documents in order can be beneficial.

Application Fees

Be prepared to pay the non-refundable application fee, which is around $107 in Pennsylvania. This fee covers the cost of processing your application and is usually payable by check, money order, or online payment methods.

- Online vs. Paper Application

Online Application

Pennsylvania offers an online application portal, which is the quickest and most convenient way to submit your application. The portal provides step-by-step instructions and allows you to upload all required documents.

Steps for Online Application:

1. Create an Account: Visit the Pennsylvania Real Estate Commission's website and create an account.
2. Fill Out the Application: Complete all sections, providing accurate and truthful information.
3. Upload Documents: Attach all required documents in the specified formats.
4. Pay the Fee: Make the payment using a credit card or other accepted online payment methods.
5. Submit: Review your application for accuracy and submit it.

Paper Application

While online applications are encouraged for their efficiency, paper applications are also accepted. These are usually downloadable from the Commission's website.

Steps for Paper Application:

1. Download the Form: Visit the Commission's website and download the application form.
2. Complete the Form: Fill it out carefully, adhering to all instructions.
3. Attach Documents: Include photocopies of all required documents.
4. Payment: Attach a check or money order for the application fee.
5. Mail: Send the completed application to the Pennsylvania Real Estate Commission's office.

- The Review Process

Initial Review

Once your application is received, it undergoes an initial review to ensure all documents are in order and the fee has been paid. Missing any of these can result in delays or outright rejection.

Background Check Verification

The Commission will verify the background check and fingerprinting results you've submitted. Any discrepancies could lead to further investigation.

Educational Requirements

Your educational certificates will be reviewed to confirm that you've met the pre-license education requirements. Make sure that the school you attended is approved by the Commission to avoid any issues.

- Common Pitfalls and How to Avoid Them

Incomplete Applications

One of the most common reasons for application delays is incomplete submissions. Double-check that you've filled out every section and attached all required documents.

Incorrect Fee Payment

Submitting the wrong amount for the application fee can result in delays. Always check the latest fee structure on the Commission's website.

Failure to Disclose

Not disclosing criminal history or other required information can lead to disqualification. Always be transparent and honest in your application.

- Special Circumstances

Reciprocity

If you're already licensed in another state with which Pennsylvania has a reciprocity agreement, you may be eligible for an expedited application process. However, you'll still need to meet Pennsylvania's specific eligibility criteria.

Military and Spouses

Special accommodations may be available for military personnel and their spouses, such as fee waivers or expedited processing. Check the Commission's website for more details.

- Final Steps

License Issuance

Once your application is approved, you'll receive your Pennsylvania real estate license. This usually takes 4-6 weeks from the date of approval.

License Activation

Your license isn't active until you're employed by a broker. You'll need to submit an additional form, signed by your employing broker, to activate your license.

- Conclusion

The application process for a real estate license in Pennsylvania is a detailed and often complex procedure. However, with careful preparation and a thorough understanding of the requirements, you can navigate it successfully. This chapter has aimed to provide a comprehensive guide to help you do just that, ensuring that you're well-equipped to take the next big step in your real estate career.

Exam Format

The Pennsylvania Real Estate License Exam is a critical milestone on your path to becoming a licensed real estate agent in the state. Understanding the exam format is crucial for effective preparation and, ultimately, for passing the test. This chapter aims to provide an in-depth look at the exam format, the types of questions you'll encounter, and the strategies you can employ to maximize your chances of success.

- Overview of the Exam

Structure

The Pennsylvania Real Estate License Exam is divided into two main sections:

National Portion: This section covers general real estate principles and practices that are applicable across the United States.
State-Specific Portion: This section focuses on real estate laws, regulations, and practices specific to Pennsylvania.

Each section has its own set of multiple-choice questions, and you must pass both sections to obtain your license.

Duration and Number of Questions

National Portion: 80 questions, 120 minutes
State-Specific Portion: 30 questions, 45 minutes

Passing Score

The passing score for each section is usually around 70-75%, but it's advisable to aim for a much higher score to ensure you pass.

- Types of Questions

Recall

These questions test your ability to remember facts and figures, such as the number of days within which a specific action must be taken according to Pennsylvania law.

Application

These questions require you to apply your knowledge to specific scenarios. For instance, you might be asked to determine the correct course of action when handling escrow funds.

Analysis

These are the most complex questions, requiring you to analyze information, draw conclusions, and make judgments based on your understanding of real estate principles and Pennsylvania law.

- Exam Topics

National Portion

1. Property Ownership and Land Use Controls
2. Laws of Agency and Fiduciary Duties
3. Property Valuation and Financial Analysis
4. Financing
5. Transfer of Property
6. Practice of Real Estate and Disclosures
7. Contracts

8. Real Estate Calculations

9. Specialty Areas

10. Ethics and Legal Considerations

State-Specific Portion

1. Licensing Requirements

2. Statutes and Rules Governing Licensee Conduct

3. Statutes and Rules Governing Agency Relationships

4. State-Specific Contract Laws

- Test-Taking Strategies

Time Management

Allocate your time wisely. It's generally a good idea to spend no more than 1-2 minutes on each question in the National Portion and about 1.5 minutes on each question in the State-Specific Portion.

Elimination Technique

If you're unsure about an answer, try to eliminate the obviously incorrect options first. This increases your chances of selecting the correct answer.

Flagging Questions

Most exam formats allow you to flag questions for review. If you're unsure about a question, flag it and move on. Return to it later if time permits.

- Special Accommodations

If you have a disability that requires special accommodations, you'll need to apply for these well in advance. Documentation verifying the disability may be required.

- What to Bring to the Exam

1. Identification: Two forms of ID, one of which must be government-issued and photo-bearing.

2. Confirmation Letter: Your exam confirmation letter or email.

3. Calculator: A simple calculator without programmable memory is usually allowed.

What Not to Bring

1. Electronic Devices: Cell phones, smartwatches, etc., are not allowed.

2. Notes or Study Materials: These are strictly prohibited and can result in disqualification.

- After the Exam

You'll receive a score report immediately upon completion of the exam. If you pass, you'll receive instructions on the next steps for obtaining your license. If you fail, you'll receive a diagnostic report indicating your strengths and weaknesses.

- Conclusion

Understanding the format of the Pennsylvania Real Estate License Exam is crucial for effective preparation and success. This chapter has aimed to provide a comprehensive guide to the exam's structure, question types, and strategies for success. With this knowledge in hand, you're well-equipped to tackle the exam and move one step closer to your career in real estate.

Property Ownership and Land Use Controls

Understanding property ownership and land use controls is not just a requirement for passing the Pennsylvania Real Estate License Exam; it's also crucial for your future career in real estate. This chapter will offer a more in-depth look into the types of property ownership, the various land use regulations, and the rights and responsibilities that come with owning property. We'll also explore the legal considerations and financial implications of these topics.

- Types of Property Ownership

Fee Simple Absolute

This is the most straightforward form of ownership. The owner has the right to control, use, and transfer the property at will. However, even fee simple ownership is subject to governmental powers like taxation, eminent domain, and police power.

Subtypes of Fee Simple Absolute
Fee Simple Defeasible: The ownership can be annulled if certain conditions are not met.
Fee Simple Determinable: The property reverts to the original owner if specific conditions are violated.

Life Estate

A life estate is a more complex form of ownership. The life tenant has the right to possess and use the property during their lifetime, but they cannot sell the property outright.

Pur Autre Vie
This is a life estate that is based on the life of a third party. It's often used in cases of life care arrangements.

Leasehold Estate

Leasehold estates are temporary in nature. They can be further divided into:

Estate for Years: A lease for a specific period.
Periodic Estate: Month-to-month or week-to-week leases.
Estate at Will: Either party can terminate the lease at any time.
Estate at Sufferance: The tenant remains on the property without the owner's consent.

Concurrent Ownership

Joint Tenancy

In a joint tenancy, each tenant has an equal right to the property. If one tenant dies, their share is divided among the surviving tenants.

Tenancy in Common

Each tenant owns a separate share of the property and can sell or transfer their share independently.

Tenancy by the Entirety

This is a form of ownership reserved for married couples. It includes the right of survivorship, meaning if one spouse dies, the surviving spouse automatically inherits the deceased spouse's share.

Land Use Controls

Zoning Laws

Zoning laws can be quite complex, and they vary from one jurisdiction to another. They can be categorized into:

Residential Zones: These are areas designated for homes and may include restrictions on the type of homes that can be built.
Commercial Zones: These are areas where business activities are allowed.
Industrial Zones: These are areas designated for manufacturing and other industrial uses.
Agricultural Zones: These are areas set aside for farming and other agricultural activities.

Building Codes

Building codes are established to ensure the safety, health, and general welfare of the public. They cover various aspects like structural integrity, electrical systems, plumbing, and fire safety.

Environmental Restrictions

These restrictions are put in place to protect the environment. They may include:

Wetlands Regulations: Limitations on what can be built near bodies of water.
Endangered Species Act: Restrictions on land use to protect endangered species.

Eminent Domain

The government's right to take private property for public use is a complex process that involves valuation and compensation. Property owners have the right to contest the amount offered as "just compensation."

Deed Restrictions and Covenants

These are private agreements that restrict the use of the property. They can be quite specific, limiting the color you can paint your house or the type of landscaping you can do.

- Rights and Responsibilities of Property Owners

Air and Mineral Rights

The rights to the air above and the minerals below the property can be sold separately from the land itself. However, there are federal and state laws that can restrict these rights.

Water Rights

The rights to use adjacent bodies of water are usually determined by state law and can be quite complex.

Right to Exclude

This is a fundamental property right, but it's not absolute. Law enforcement officers may enter your property under specific conditions, and utility companies may have easements that allow them access to certain parts of your property.

Right to Transfer

This is the right to sell, lease, or will your property, but it's subject to federal and state laws, as well as any existing deed restrictions.

Responsibilities

Owning property comes with responsibilities like paying property taxes, maintaining the property, and adhering to zoning regulations and building codes.

- Conclusion

Understanding property ownership and land use controls is a multi-faceted subject that involves legal, financial, and ethical considerations. This chapter has aimed to provide a comprehensive and in-depth overview, equipping you with the knowledge you need to navigate the complex landscape of property ownership and land use in Pennsylvania.

Mock Exam Property Ownership and Land Use Controls

1. What is the most straightforward form of property ownership?

A. Life Estate
B. Leasehold Estate
C. Fee Simple Absolute
D. Joint Tenancy

Answer: C

Fee Simple Absolute is the most straightforward form of property ownership, offering the most extensive rights to the owner.

2. Which type of estate is temporary in nature?

A. Fee Simple Absolute
B. Life Estate
C. Leasehold Estate
D. Joint Tenancy

Answer: C

Leasehold estates are temporary and do not provide the lessee with ownership of the property.

3. What is the primary purpose of zoning laws?

A. To collect taxes
B. To regulate land use
C. To establish building codes
D. To protect endangered species

Answer: B

Zoning laws are designed to regulate land use within a jurisdiction.

4. Which of the following is a private agreement that restricts the use of property?

  A. Zoning Law
  B. Building Code
  C. Deed Restriction
  D. Eminent Domain

Answer: C

Deed restrictions are private agreements that limit the use of the property.

5. What is the right of the government to take private property for public use?

  A. Police Power
  B. Eminent Domain
  C. Taxation
  D. Escheat

Answer: B

Eminent Domain is the government's right to take private property for public use.

6. Which type of ownership is reserved for married couples?

  A. Joint Tenancy
  B. Tenancy in Common
  C. Tenancy by the Entirety
  D. Community Property

Answer: C

Tenancy by the Entirety is a form of ownership reserved for married couples.

➟7. What is a life estate based on the life of a third party called?

   A. Life Estate Pur Autre Vie
   B. Life Estate Remainder
   C. Life Estate Reversion
   D. Life Estate Absolute

Answer: A
A life estate based on the life of a third party is called Life Estate Pur Autre Vie.

➟8. Which of the following is NOT a governmental power affecting property ownership?

   A. Taxation
   B. Eminent Domain
   C. Escheat
   D. Deed Restriction

Answer: D
  Deed Restriction is a private agreement, not a governmental power.

➟9. What is the primary purpose of building codes?

   A. To regulate land use
   B. To ensure public safety
   C. To collect taxes
   D. To protect property values

Answer: B
Building codes are established to ensure the safety, health, and general welfare of the public.

→ 10. Which of the following is a restriction put in place to protect the environment?

A. Wetlands Regulations
B. Zoning Laws
C. Building Codes
D. Deed Restrictions

Answer: A

Wetlands Regulations are put in place to protect the environment, particularly bodies of water.

→ 11. What is the right to use adjacent bodies of water usually determined by?

A. Federal Law
B. State Law
C. Local Ordinances
D. Deed Restrictions

Answer: B

Water rights are usually determined by state law.

→ 12. Which of the following is NOT a subtype of Fee Simple Absolute?

A. Fee Simple Defeasible
B. Fee Simple Determinable
C. Fee Simple Conditional
D. Fee Simple Reversionary

Answer: D

Fee Simple Reversionary is not a subtype of Fee Simple Absolute.

What is the right to sell, lease, or will your property subject to?

A. Only Federal Laws
B. Only State Laws
C. Federal and State Laws
D. Deed Restrictions Only

Answer: C

The right to transfer property is subject to both federal and state laws, as well as any existing deed restrictions.

➡14. Which of the following is a form of concurrent ownership?

A. Tenancy by the Entirety
B. Life Estate
C. Leasehold Estate
D. Fee Simple Absolute

Answer: A

Tenancy by the Entirety is a form of concurrent ownership.

➡15. What is the right to exclude others from your property?

A. Right of Survivorship
B. Right to Transfer
C. Right to Exclude
D. Right to Use

Answer: C

The right to exclude is a fundamental property right, allowing the owner to keep others off their property.

→16. What is the primary difference between a life estate and a fee simple estate?

  A. Transferability
  B. Duration
  C. Ownership rights
  D. Tax implications

Answer: B

The primary difference is the duration; a life estate lasts for the lifetime of the owner or another designated person, while a fee simple estate is indefinite.

→17. What is the legal process by which the government takes private land for public use?

  A. Confiscation
  B. Condemnation
  C. Seizure
  D. Requisition

Answer: B

Condemnation is the legal process by which the government exercises its power of eminent domain.

→18. What is the primary purpose of a variance in zoning laws?

  A. To change the zoning classification
  B. To allow an exception to current zoning laws
  C. To enforce building codes
  D. To protect natural resources

Answer: B
A variance allows for an exception to current zoning laws for a specific property.

➡19. What is the right to use someone else's land for a specific purpose called?

A. Easement
B. Leasehold
C. Encroachment
D. Lien

Answer: A

An easement allows one to use another's land for a specific purpose, like a driveway or utility lines.

➡20. What is the term for a restriction on the maximum number of buildings that can be built on a certain area of land?

A. Density Zoning
B. Bulk Zoning
C. Aesthetic Zoning
D. Incentive Zoning

Answer: A

Density zoning restricts the maximum number of buildings on a specific area of land.

➡21. What is the term for the right of a government or its agent to expropriate private property for public use, with payment of compensation?

A. Police Power
B. Eminent Domain
C. Escheat
D. Taxation

Answer: B

Eminent Domain is the right to expropriate private property for public use with compensation.

→22. What is the term for a legal claim against a property that must be paid off when the property is sold?

A. Easement
B. Lien
C. Encumbrance
D. Deed Restriction

Answer: B

A lien is a legal claim against a property that must be paid off when the property is sold.

→23. What is the term for the rights to use, enjoy, and dispose of a property in any legal way?

A. Bundle of Rights
B. Property Rights
C. Ownership Rights
D. Legal Rights

Answer: A

The term "Bundle of Rights" refers to the legal rights of the property owner to use, enjoy, and dispose of the property.

→24. What is the term for a legal way to use property in a manner that is contrary to local zoning laws?

A. Nonconforming Use
B. Illegal Use

Variance

. Special Use Permit

Answer: A

Nonconforming Use is a legal way to use property that does not conform to current zoning laws.

➡ 25. What is the term for a legal agreement that controls the use of land?

A. Deed Restriction
B. Easement
C. Lien
D. Encumbrance

Answer: A

A Deed Restriction is a legal agreement that controls the use of the land.

➡ 26. What is the primary purpose of a building permit?

A. To grant permission for new construction or alterations
B. To change zoning laws
C. To enforce property taxes
D. To grant ownership rights

Answer: A

A building permit grants permission for new construction or alterations, ensuring that they comply with local building codes.

➡ 27. What is the term for the rights to natural resources like minerals, water, and air space on a property?

A. Surface Rights

B. Air Rights

C. Subsurface Rights

D. Riparian Rights

Answer: C

Subsurface Rights pertain to the natural resources found beneath the surface of the property.

28. What is the term for the right to use a body of water adjacent to a property?

A. Littoral Rights

B. Riparian Rights

C. Water Rights

D. Surface Rights

Answer: B

Riparian Rights are the rights to use a body of water adjacent to a property.

29. What is the term for a property that is free from any encumbrances or restrictions?

A. Freehold

B. Unencumbered

C. Fee Simple

D. Clear Title

Answer: B

An unencumbered property is free from any encumbrances or restrictions.

30. What is the term for a legal restriction on the height of a building?

A. Height Restriction

B. Bulk Zoning

C. Density Zoning

D. Setback

Answer: B

Bulk Zoning includes restrictions on the height of buildings.

31. What is the term for a property that is used in a way that violates local zoning laws but is allowed to continue because it existed before the laws were enacted?

A. Grandfathered Use

B. Nonconforming Use

C. Variance

D. Special Use Permit

Answer: B

Nonconforming Use refers to a property that violates current zoning laws but is allowed to continue because it existed before the laws were enacted.

32. What is the term for a legal agreement between a landowner and a public body to restrict the use of land in perpetuity?

A. Conservation Easement

B. Restrictive Covenant

C. Zoning Ordinance

D. Deed Restriction

Answer: A

A Conservation Easement is a legal agreement to restrict the use of land to protect its conservation values.

➡33. What is the term for a property that has multiple owners, each with a percentage of ownership?

A. Joint Tenancy
B. Tenancy in Common
C. Condominium
D. Cooperative

Answer: B

Tenancy in Common refers to a property with multiple owners, each owning a specific percentage.

➡34. What is the term for a property that is owned by one entity but is made up of individual units that are leased?

A. Condominium
B. Cooperative
C. Joint Tenancy
D. Tenancy in Common

Answer: B

In a Cooperative, the property is owned by one entity, and individual units are leased to residents.

➡35. What is the term for the right of a property owner to convert real property into personal property by detaching it from the land?

A. Severance
B. Attachment
C. Conversion
D. Alienation

Answer: A

Severance is the right to convert real property into personal property by detaching it from the land.

➡ 36. What is the term for a property that is owned by a single entity and rented out to tenants?

   A. Single-Family Home
   B. Multi-Family Home
   C. Condominium
   D. Apartment Building

Answer: D

An apartment building is owned by a single entity and rented out to tenants.

➡ 37. What is the term for a property that is owned by two or more people without the right of survivorship?

   A. Joint Tenancy
   B. Tenancy in Common
   C. Condominium
   D. Cooperative

Answer: B

Tenancy in Common refers to a property owned by two or more people without the right of survivorship.

➡ 38. What is the term for a property that is owned by a single person or entity?

   A. Sole Ownership
   B. Joint Tenancy

C. Tenancy in Common

D. Cooperative

Answer: A

Sole Ownership refers to a property owned by a single person or entity.

➡ 39. What is the term for a property that is owned by a married couple?

A. Tenancy by the Entirety

B. Joint Tenancy

C. Tenancy in Common

D. Sole Ownership

Answer: A

Tenancy by the Entirety refers to a property owned by a married couple.

➡ 40. What is the term for a property that is owned by a group of people who share common interests?

A. Cooperative

B. Condominium

C. Tenancy in Common

D. Joint Tenancy

Answer: A

A Cooperative is owned by a group of people who share common interests.

➡ 41. What is the term for the right of a government to acquire property that has been abandoned for a certain period?

A. Eminent Domain

B. Adverse Possession

C. Escheat

D. Foreclosure

Answer: C

Escheat is the right of a government to acquire property that has been abandoned for a certain period.

➡ 42. What is the term for the right to use someone else's land for a specific purpose?

A. Easement

B. Leasehold

C. Lien

D. Encroachment

Answer: A

An easement grants the right to use someone else's land for a specific purpose.

➡ 43. What is the term for a restriction on how a property may be used, often set by the developer?

A. Covenant

B. Easement

C. Zoning

D. Encroachment

Answer: A

A covenant is a restriction on how a property may be used, often set by the developer.

➡ 44. What is the term for a property that is owned and managed by a homeowners' association?

A. Cooperative

B. Condominium

C. Planned Unit Development

D. Apartment Building

Answer: C

A Planned Unit Development is owned and managed by a homeowners' association.

➡ 45. What is the term for a legal claim against a property for unpaid debt?

A. Lien

B. Easement

C. Encroachment

D. Covenant

Answer: A

A lien is a legal claim against a property for unpaid debt.

➡ 46. What is the term for a property that is owned by two or more people with the right of survivorship?

A. Joint Tenancy

B. Tenancy in Common

C. Sole Ownership

D. Tenancy by the Entirety

Answer: A

Joint Tenancy refers to a property owned by two or more people with the right of survivorship.

➡ 47. What is the term for a property that is owned by a corporation, and residents own shares in the corporation?

A. Cooperative
B. Condominium
C. Apartment Building
D. Planned Unit Development

Answer: A

A Cooperative is owned by a corporation, and residents own shares in the corporation.

➡ 48. What is the term for a property that is owned by an individual who rents out individual units?

A. Apartment Building
B. Condominium
C. Cooperative
D. Planned Unit Development

Answer: B

A Condominium is owned by an individual who rents out individual units.

➡ 49. What is the term for a property that is owned by a single entity and consists of multiple units?

A. Apartment Building
B. Condominium
C. Cooperative
D. Planned Unit Development

Answer: A

An Apartment Building is owned by a single entity and consists of multiple units.

➡ 50. What is the term for a property that is owned by a single entity and is rented out to multiple tenants?

A. Apartment Building
B. Condominium
C. Cooperative
D. Planned Unit Development

Answer: A

An Apartment Building is owned by a single entity and is rented out to multiple tenants.

Laws of Agency and Fiduciary Duties

The real estate industry is a complex web of relationships, transactions, and legal obligations. At the core of this intricate system is the concept of agency, which defines the relationship between a real estate agent and their client. This chapter aims to provide an in-depth understanding of agency laws and fiduciary duties in Pennsylvania, offering a detailed guide for both new and experienced real estate professionals.

- Types of Agency Relationships

Seller's Agent

When you list your property for sale, the agent you hire is known as a seller's agent. This agent owes you fiduciary duties, which means they must act in your best interest throughout the transaction. They are responsible for marketing your property, negotiating on your behalf, and guiding you through the closing process.

Responsibilities of a Seller's Agent
- *Market Analysis*
- *Property Staging*
- *Advertising*
- *Open Houses*
- *Negotiation*
- *Closing Procedures*

Buyer's Agent

A buyer's agent represents the buyer in a real estate transaction. They owe fiduciary duties to the buyer, which means they must act in the buyer's best interest. They assist the buyer in finding a suitable property, negotiating the price, and navigating the closing process.

Responsibilities of a Buyer's Agent
- *Property Search*
- *Comparative Market Analysis*
- *Offer Preparation*
- *Negotiation*
- *Inspection Coordination*
- *Closing Procedures*

Dual Agency

Dual agency occurs when an agent represents both the buyer and the seller in the same transaction. This is a complex situation that requires the informed consent of both parties. The agent must balance the interests of both parties, which can be challenging.

Ethical and Legal Challenges
- *Conflict of Interest*
- *Informed Consent*
- *Disclosure Requirements*
- *Limitations on Advocacy*

Subagency

Subagency usually occurs within the same brokerage. One agent may delegate some of their responsibilities to another agent, but both owe fiduciary duties to the original client.

How Subagency Works
- *Delegation of Duties*
- *Shared Responsibilities*
- *Legal Obligations*

- Fiduciary Duties

Loyalty

The agent must always act in the best interest of their client. This means putting the client's needs above their own and avoiding conflicts of interest.

Case Studies on Loyalty

- *Example 1: An agent prioritizes their commission over the client's best price.*
- *Example 2: An agent discloses confidential information to benefit themselves.*

Disclosure

Full transparency is crucial in any agency relationship. Agents must disclose all material facts that could influence the client's decisions.

Importance of Timely Disclosure

- *Legal Requirements*
- *Ethical Considerations*
- *Case Studies*

Confidentiality

Maintaining confidentiality is not just an ethical obligation but also a legal one. Agents must protect their client's personal and financial information.

What Constitutes Confidential Information?

- *Financial Status*
- *Motivation for Buying/Selling*
- *Personal Circumstances*

Obedience, Reasonable Care and Diligence, and Accounting

These duties require the agent to follow all lawful instructions, act competently and diligently, and account for all funds and property received during the agency relationship.

- Legal Considerations

Disclosure Requirements

Pennsylvania law mandates that agents must disclose their agency status through an agency disclosure form. Failure to do so can result in legal consequences.

Termination of Agency

Agency relationships can end for various reasons, including the completion of a transaction, expiration of an agreement, or mutual consent. It's crucial to understand the legal implications of terminating an agency relationship.

Violations and Penalties

Agents who fail to adhere to agency laws and fiduciary duties may face disciplinary actions, including fines, license suspension, or revocation.

- Ethical Considerations

The National Association of Realtors (NAR) has a Code of Ethics that supplements state laws, providing additional guidelines for ethical conduct. Violating these can result in disciplinary action from the association.

- Conclusion

Understanding the laws of agency and fiduciary duties is not just essential for passing the real estate exam but also for a successful career in this field. This chapter has aimed to provide a comprehensive guide to these critical aspects of real estate practice in Pennsylvania.

By adhering to these principles and guidelines, you not only protect your clients but also yourself from legal repercussions. It sets the foundation for a successful, ethical, and rewarding career in real estate.

Mock Exam Laws of Agency and Fiduciary Duties

1. What is the primary duty of a seller's agent?

A. To find the highest bidder
B. To act in the seller's best interest
C. To close the deal as quickly as possible
D. To represent both parties fairly

Answer: B

The primary duty of a seller's agent is to act in the seller's best interest, fulfilling their fiduciary duties.

2. Which of the following is NOT a fiduciary duty?

A. Loyalty
B. Disclosure
C. Profit maximization
D. Confidentiality

Answer: C

Profit maximization is not considered a fiduciary duty. The fiduciary duties are loyalty, disclosure, and confidentiality among others.

3. What is dual agency?

A. When two agents represent the seller
B. When an agent represents both buyer and seller
C. When two agencies collaborate on a deal
D. When an agent represents two buyers

Answer: B

Dual agency occurs when an agent represents both the buyer and the seller in the same transaction.

➡ 4. What is required for dual agency to be ethical?

A. Verbal agreement from both parties
B. Written consent from both parties
C. Dual agency is never ethical
D. A higher commission for the agent

Answer: B

Dual agency requires the informed, written consent of both parties to be considered ethical.

➡ 5. What does the term "subagency" refer to?

A. An agency within an agency
B. When an agent delegates duties to another agent
C. A temporary agency relationship
D. An agency that works under another agency

Answer: B

Subagency usually occurs when one agent delegates some of their responsibilities to another agent within the same brokerage.

➡ 6. Which of the following is considered confidential information?

A. The seller's asking price
B. The buyer's financial status
C. The commission rate of the agent
D. The listing price of the property

Answer: B

The buyer's financial status is considered confidential information that the agent must protect.

7. What is the primary focus of the National Association of Realtors' Code of Ethics?

A. Profit maximization
B. Legal compliance
C. Ethical conduct
D. Marketing strategies

Answer: C

The primary focus of the NAR's Code of Ethics is to provide guidelines for ethical conduct among its members.

8. What happens if an agent fails to disclose their agency status in Pennsylvania?

A. A warning is issued
B. The deal is nullified
C. Legal consequences
D. The agent is promoted

Answer: C

Failure to disclose agency status can result in legal consequences, including fines and potential license suspension.

9. Which fiduciary duty requires an agent to act competently and diligently?

A. Loyalty

B. Obedience

C. Reasonable Care and Diligence

D. Accounting

Answer: C

The duty of Reasonable Care and Diligence requires the agent to act competently and diligently on behalf of their client.

➡10. What is the primary duty of a buyer's agent?

A. To find the lowest price for the property

B. To act in the buyer's best interest

C. To close the deal as quickly as possible

D. To represent both parties fairly

Answer: B

The primary duty of a buyer's agent is to act in the buyer's best interest, fulfilling their fiduciary duties.

➡11. What is the "Implied Agency" in real estate?

A. An agency relationship that is written and signed

B. An agency relationship that is assumed but not written

C. An agency relationship that is illegal

D. An agency relationship that is temporary

Answer: B

Implied Agency is an agency relationship that exists based on the behavior of the parties, even though it's not written down.

➡12. What is the agent required to do under the fiduciary duty of "Accounting"?

A. Keep track of all financial transactions

B. Act in the best interest of the client

C. Keep all information confidential

D. Disclose all known facts about the property

Answer: A

The fiduciary duty of "Accounting" requires the agent to keep accurate records of all financial transactions related to the agency relationship.

13. What does the "Universal Agent" have the power to do?

A. Represent multiple clients at once

B. Perform any act the principal could perform

C. Only represent the client in real estate transactions

D. Represent the client in a single transaction

Answer: B

A Universal Agent has the power to perform any and all acts that can be legally delegated by the principal.

14. What is "Designated Agency"?

A. When an agent represents both parties

B. When an agent represents only the buyer

C. When a broker designates agents to represent different parties

D. When an agent represents only the seller

Answer: C

Designated Agency occurs when the broker designates different agents within the same brokerage to represent the buyer and the seller.

15. What is the consequence of violating a fiduciary duty?

A. Loss of commission

B. Legal repercussions

C. A warning letter

D. No consequences

Answer: B

Violating a fiduciary duty can lead to legal repercussions, including lawsuits and potential loss of license.

16. What is the purpose of a "Buyer's Agency Agreement"?

A. To outline the duties of the seller's agent

B. To outline the duties of the buyer's agent

C. To finalize the sale of the property

D. To establish dual agency

Answer: B

A Buyer's Agency Agreement outlines the responsibilities and duties of the agent towards the buyer.

17. What is "Single Agency"?

A. Representing both the buyer and seller

B. Representing only one party in the transaction

C. Representing multiple buyers

D. Representing multiple sellers

Answer: B

Single Agency means the agent represents only one party in the transaction, either the buyer or the seller.

18. What is "Transaction Brokerage"?

A. When a broker represents both parties
B. When a broker represents neither party
C. When a broker represents only the buyer
D. When a broker represents only the seller

Answer: B

In Transaction Brokerage, the broker does not represent either party but facilitates the transaction.

➡19. What is the agent's responsibility under the duty of "Disclosure"?

A. To reveal all known material facts
B. To keep all information confidential
C. To act in the best interest of the client
D. To account for all financial transactions

Answer: A

Under the duty of "Disclosure," the agent is required to reveal all known material facts relevant to the transaction.

➡20. What is the "Special Agent" authorized to do?

A. Perform any act the principal could perform
B. Represent the client in a specific transaction
C. Represent multiple clients at once
D. Act without the principal's consent

Answer: B

A Special Agent is authorized to represent the client in a specific transaction but does not have the broad powers that a Universal Agent would have.

21. What is the primary role of a "Subagent"?

A. To represent the buyer
B. To represent the seller
C. To assist the principal agent in representing the client
D. To act as a neutral third party

Answer: C

A Subagent assists the principal agent in carrying out the responsibilities towards the client, usually the seller.

22. What does the fiduciary duty of "Loyalty" require?

A. Disclosing all material facts
B. Acting in the best interest of the client
C. Keeping accurate financial records
D. Keeping all client information confidential

Answer: B

The duty of "Loyalty" requires the agent to act in the best interest of the client above all others, including themselves.

23. What is "Dual Agency"?

A. Representing only the buyer
B. Representing only the seller
C. Representing both the buyer and seller in the same transaction
D. Representing neither the buyer nor the seller

Answer: C

Dual Agency occurs when an agent represents both the buyer and the seller in the same transaction, which can present a conflict of interest.

24. What is the agent's responsibility under the duty of "Obedience"?

A. To follow all lawful instructions from the client
B. To disclose all material facts
C. To act in the best interest of the client
D. To keep all client information confidential

Answer: A

The duty of "Obedience" requires the agent to follow all lawful instructions given by the client.

25. What is the "Listing Agreement" primarily used for?

A. To outline the buyer's agent duties
B. To outline the seller's agent duties
C. To finalize the sale of the property
D. To establish dual agency

Answer: B

A Listing Agreement is a contract that outlines the responsibilities and duties of the agent towards the seller.

26. What does the fiduciary duty of "Confidentiality" require?

A. Disclosing all material facts
B. Acting in the best interest of the client
C. Keeping all client information confidential
D. Keeping accurate financial records

Answer: C

The duty of "Confidentiality" requires the agent to keep all client information confidential, even after the agency relationship has ended.

27. What is a "Client" in a real estate agency relationship?

A. The person represented by the agent
B. The person selling the property
C. The person buying the property
D. The person who is a subagent

Answer: A

A Client is the person who is represented by the agent in the agency relationship, either as a buyer or a seller.

28. What is "Express Agency"?

A. An agency relationship that is assumed but not written
B. An agency relationship that is written and signed
C. An agency relationship that is illegal
D. An agency relationship that is temporary

Answer: B

Express Agency is an agency relationship that is formally written and signed by both parties.

29. What is the agent's responsibility under the duty of "Reasonable Care"?

A. To act competently and carefully
B. To disclose all material facts
C. To act in the best interest of the client
D. To keep all client information confidential

Answer: A

The duty of "Reasonable Care" requires the agent to act competently and carefully in representing the client.

➡ 30. What is "Termination of Agency"?

A. When an agent takes on a new client
B. When an agency relationship ends
C. When an agent represents both parties
D. When an agent violates fiduciary duties

Answer: B

Termination of Agency occurs when the agency relationship between the agent and the client ends, either due to the fulfillment of the agency's purpose or other reasons.

➡ 31. What is the primary purpose of a "Buyer's Agent"?

A. To represent the seller
B. To represent the buyer
C. To assist the listing agent
D. To act as a neutral third party

Answer: B

A Buyer's Agent is specifically tasked with representing the interests of the buyer in a real estate transaction.

➡ 32. What does the fiduciary duty of "Accounting" require?

A. Disclosing all material facts
B. Keeping accurate financial records
C. Acting in the best interest of the client
D. Keeping all client information confidential

Answer: B

The duty of "Accounting" requires the agent to keep accurate financial records related to the transaction.

33. What is "Implied Agency"?

A. An agency relationship that is written and signed

B. An agency relationship that is assumed but not written

C. An agency relationship that is illegal

D. An agency relationship that is temporary

Answer: B

Implied Agency is an agency relationship that exists based on the behavior of the parties, even though it's not written down.

34. What is the agent's responsibility under the duty of "Loyalty"?

A. To act in the best interest of the client

B. To disclose all material facts

C. To keep all client information confidential

D. To follow all lawful instructions from the client

Answer: A

The duty of "Loyalty" requires the agent to act in the best interest of the client, above all others, including themselves.

35. What is a "Transaction Broker"?

A. Represents only the buyer

B. Represents only the seller

C. Represents both the buyer and seller

D. Represents neither the buyer nor the seller

Answer: D

A Transaction Broker facilitates the transaction without representing either party's interests.

➙36. What does the fiduciary duty of "Honesty" require?

A. Disclosing all material facts
B. Acting in the best interest of the client
C. Keeping all client information confidential
D. Being truthful in all dealings

Answer: D

The duty of "Honesty" requires the agent to be truthful in all dealings with the client and other parties involved in the transaction.

➙37. What is a "Single Agency"?

A. Representing only the buyer
B. Representing only the seller
C. Representing both the buyer and seller
D. Representing neither the buyer nor the seller

Answer: A or B

Single Agency is when an agent represents only one party in a transaction, either the buyer or the seller.

➙38. What is the agent's responsibility under the duty of "Skill and Care"?

A. To act competently and carefully
B. To disclose all material facts
C. To act in the best interest of the client
D. To keep all client information confidential

Answer: A

The duty of "Skill and Care" requires the agent to act competently and carefully in representing the client.

➟39. What is "Subagency"?

A. An agency where the agent represents only the buyer

B. An agency where the agent represents only the seller

C. An agency where one agent acts on behalf of another agent in representing a client

D. An agency where both parties are represented by the same agent

Answer: C

Subagency occurs when one agent acts on behalf of another agent in representing a client, often without a direct contractual relationship with the client.

➟40. What is the agent's responsibility under the duty of "Cooperation"?

A. To work well with other agents

B. To disclose all material facts

C. To act in the best interest of the client

D. To keep all client information confidential

Answer: A

The duty of "Cooperation" requires the agent to work well with other agents to the benefit of the client.

➟41. What is the primary purpose of a "Buyer's Agency Agreement"?

A. To outline the commission structure

B. To establish the agent's fiduciary duties

C. To define the relationship between the buyer and the agent

D. To list the properties the buyer is interested in

Answer: C

The primary purpose of a "Buyer's Agency Agreement" is to define the relationship between the buyer and the agent, including the scope of the agent's duties and responsibilities.

42. What is "Imputed Notice"?

A. Information that is publicly available
B. Information that is confidential
C. Information that is assumed to be known
D. Information that is disclosed in writing

Answer: C

Imputed Notice is information that is assumed to be known, even if it has not been directly communicated.

43. What is the agent's responsibility under the duty of "Accounting"?

A. To keep accurate financial records
B. To act in the best interest of the client
C. To disclose all material facts
D. To keep all client information confidential

Answer: A

The duty of "Accounting" requires the agent to keep accurate financial records related to the transaction.

44. What does "Subagency" mean in real estate?

A. An agent representing both the buyer and the seller
B. An agent representing another agent in a transaction
C. An agent working under another agent within the same brokerage
D. An agent representing only the seller

Answer: C

Subagency refers to an agent working under another agent within the same brokerage, often assisting in tasks and responsibilities.

45. What is "Ratification" in an agency relationship?

A. The termination of the agency relationship
B. The approval of an agent's actions by the principal
C. The agent acting outside the scope of their authority
D. The agent disclosing confidential information

Answer: B

Ratification occurs when the principal approves the actions of the agent, even if those actions were initially unauthorized.

46. What is the agent's responsibility under the duty of "Reasonable Care"?

A. To act in the best interest of the client
B. To exercise competence and skill in performing tasks
C. To disclose all material facts
D. To keep all client information confidential

Answer: B

The duty of "Reasonable Care" requires the agent to exercise competence and skill in performing tasks related to the transaction.

47. What is "Constructive Notice"?

A. Information that is publicly available
B. Information that is confidential
C. Information that is assumed to be known
D. Information that is disclosed in writing

Answer: A

Constructive Notice is information that is publicly available and therefore should be known.

➡ 48. What is "Puffing" in real estate?

A. Exaggerating property features
B. Disclosing material facts
C. Acting in the best interest of the client
D. Keeping accurate financial records

Answer: A

Puffing refers to the exaggeration of property features, which is generally considered legal but can be unethical.

➡ 49. What is "Single Agency" in real estate?

A. An agency where the agent represents only the buyer
B. An agency where the agent represents only the seller
C. An agency where one agent represents both the buyer and the seller
D. An agency where different agents within the same brokerage represent the buyer and the seller

Answer: A

Single Agency is an agency where the agent represents only one party, either the buyer or the seller, but not both.

➡ 50. What is "Novation" in an agency relationship?

A. The termination of the agency relationship
B. The approval of an agent's actions by the principal
C. The substitution of a new contract or party

D. The agent disclosing confidential information

Answer: C

Novation is the substitution of a new contract or party in an existing contract, effectively replacing the terms or parties involved.

Property Valuation and Financial Analysis

The real estate industry is a complex web of transactions, negotiations, and financial planning. At the heart of it all is property valuation and financial analysis. These are the cornerstones that guide decision-making for buyers, sellers, investors, and real estate professionals alike. This chapter aims to offer an in-depth look into these critical aspects, providing you with the tools you need to navigate the complexities of the real estate market.

- Methods of Property Valuation

Comparative Market Analysis (CMA)

What is CMA?

Comparative Market Analysis is a method that involves comparing the property in question to similar properties that have recently sold in the same area. This is often the first step in determining a property's value and is commonly used for residential properties.

Factors Considered in CMA

Location: Proximity to amenities, quality of the local school district, crime rates, and future developments in the area.
Size: Square footage, number of bedrooms and bathrooms.
Condition: Age of the property, structural integrity, quality of construction, and state of repair.
Amenities: Special features like a swimming pool, garden, garage, etc.

Limitations of CMA

While CMA is useful, it has its limitations, such as not accounting for the unique characteristics that might make a property more valuable.

Cost Approach

What is the Cost Approach?

The cost approach is based on the idea that a property's value should be equal to the cost of constructing a similar property from scratch today, plus the value of the land it's on.

Components of the Cost Approach

Land Value: Determined through a process similar to CMA but focuses on land sales.
Replacement Cost: The cost of building a similar structure, factoring in current prices for labor and materials.
Depreciation: Accounting for the loss in value due to age, wear and tear, or obsolescence.

Income Approach

What is the Income Approach?

This method is often used for commercial and investment properties. It calculates the property's value based on the income it generates.

Calculating Income Value

Net Operating Income (NOI): Gross income minus operating expenses.
Capitalization Rate: The rate of return expected on an investment.

- Financial Analysis

Cash Flow Analysis

Importance of Cash Flow

Cash flow is the lifeblood of any investment property. A positive cash flow means the property is generating more income than expenses, making it a good investment.

Components of Cash Flow

Income: Rent, parking fees, laundry income, etc.
Expenses: Mortgage, taxes, insurance, maintenance, and property management fees.

Return on Investment (ROI)

Calculating ROI

ROI is calculated by taking the net profit of the investment and dividing it by the initial cost. This gives you a percentage that represents the profitability of the investment.

Factors Affecting ROI

Property Value: A higher property value can increase ROI.
Loan Terms: The terms of your mortgage can significantly impact your ROI.

Loan-to-Value Ratio (LTV)

What is LTV?

The Loan-to-Value ratio is a measure used by lenders to assess the risk associated with a mortgage. It is calculated by dividing the mortgage amount by the appraised value of the property.

Importance of LTV

A lower LTV generally means lower risk for the lender, which could translate to lower interest rates for the borrower.

- Risk Assessment

Market Risks

Economic Factors: Inflation, employment rates, and economic growth can all affect property value.

Market Demand: The number of people looking to buy or rent in the area.

Financial Risks

Interest Rates: A rise in interest rates can increase mortgage payments.

Property Taxes: An increase in property taxes can affect your cash flow.

Maintenance Costs: Older properties may require more maintenance, affecting your bottom line.

- Tax Considerations

Property Taxes: Vary by location and can be deductible.

Capital Gains Tax: Tax on the profit from the sale of a property.

Depreciation: Can be used as a tax deduction for investment properties.

Conclusion

Understanding property valuation and financial analysis is not just beneficial but essential for anyone involved in the real estate market. Whether you're a first-time homebuyer, a seasoned investor, or a real estate professional, the concepts covered in this chapter are fundamental to making informed decisions. By applying these principles, you can maximize your financial gains, minimize your risks, and navigate the complex landscape of the real estate market with confidence.

Mock Exam Property Valuation and Financial Analysis

➡ 1. What does the term "highest and best use" refer to in property valuation?

A. The most profitable use of the property
B. The most ethical use of the property
C. The use that generates the most tax revenue
D. The use that is most popular in the community

Answer: A

The term "highest and best use" refers to the most profitable use of a property, considering its current or potential zoning, market demand, and other factors.

➡ 2. What is the main focus of the Income Approach to property valuation?

A. Market demand
B. Comparable sales
C. Future income potential
D. Cost of construction

Answer: C

The main focus of the Income Approach is the future income potential of the property, often calculated using metrics like Net Operating Income and Capitalization Rate.

➡ 3. What is a "comparable" in the context of Comparative Market Analysis?

A. A similar property that has recently sold
B. A property in a different market
C. A property that is currently listed
D. A property that has been foreclosed

Answer: A

A "comparable" is a similar property that has recently sold, and is used as a basis for determining the value of the property being appraised.

➡4. What does the term "amortization" refer to in the context of mortgages?

  A. The process of increasing property value
  B. The process of paying off a loan over time
  C. The process of calculating property taxes
  D. The process of determining market demand

Answer: B

Amortization refers to the process of paying off a loan over time through regular payments, which cover both principal and interest.

➡5. What is the main disadvantage of the Cost Approach to property valuation?

  A. It is too simple
  B. It is too expensive
  C. It does not consider market demand
  D. It does not consider future income

Answer: C

The main disadvantage of the Cost Approach is that it does not consider market demand, which can significantly affect the value of a property.

➡6. What is the Loan-to-Value (LTV) ratio?

  A. The ratio of the loan amount to the property's appraised value
  B. The ratio of the loan amount to the borrower's income
  C. The ratio of the property's appraised value to the market value
  D. The ratio of the loan amount to the market value

Answer: A

The Loan-to-Value (LTV) ratio is the ratio of the loan amount to the property's appraised value. It is used by lenders to assess the risk of the loan.

➠7. What does a capitalization rate indicate?

A. The cost of constructing a property
B. The potential return on an investment property
C. The market demand for a property
D. The property's historical value

Answer: B

The capitalization rate indicates the potential return on an investment property, often used in the Income Approach to valuation.

➠8. What is the purpose of a "subject property" in Comparative Market Analysis?

A. To serve as a benchmark for comparison
B. To serve as the property being appraised
C. To serve as a recently sold property
D. To serve as a property in foreclosure

Answer: B

The "subject property" is the property being appraised in Comparative Market Analysis.

➠9. What does "net operating income" (NOI) represent?

A. Gross income minus operating expenses
B. Gross income minus taxes
C. Gross income minus mortgage payments
D. Gross income minus depreciation

Answer: A

Net Operating Income (NOI) represents the gross income of a property minus its operating expenses, not including mortgage payments or depreciation.

10. What is the primary focus of the Sales Comparison Approach?

A. Future income potential
B. Cost of construction
C. Comparable sales
D. Market demand

Answer: C

The primary focus of the Sales Comparison Approach is comparable sales, using them to determine the value of the property being appraised.

11. What is "equity" in the context of real estate?

A. The market value of a property
B. The difference between the property's market value and the outstanding loan amount
C. The initial down payment on a property
D. The annual property tax

Answer: B

Equity is the difference between the property's market value and the outstanding loan amount.

12. What does "cash flow" refer to in real estate investment?

A. The total income generated by a property
B. The net income after all expenses and mortgage payments
C. The annual property tax

D. The initial down payment

Answer: B

Cash flow refers to the net income generated by a property after all expenses and mortgage payments have been deducted.

13. What is a "contingency" in a real estate deal?

A. A legal requirement
B. A future event that could affect the deal
C. A penalty for late payment
D. A type of mortgage

Answer: B

A contingency is a future event or condition that could affect the real estate deal, such as a home inspection or financing.

14. What does "due diligence" refer to in real estate transactions?

A. The process of verifying all aspects of a deal
B. The process of securing financing
C. The process of home inspection
D. The process of title search

Answer: A

Due diligence refers to the process of verifying all aspects of a real estate deal, including legal, financial, and physical aspects.

15. What is "escrow" in the context of real estate?

A. A legal agreement between buyer and seller

B. A neutral third party holding funds or documents

C. A type of mortgage

D. A future event that could affect the deal

Answer: B

Escrow refers to a neutral third party holding funds or documents until the conditions of a real estate deal are met.

16. What does "amortization" refer to in real estate financing?

A. The process of paying off a loan over time

B. The process of increasing property value

C. The process of calculating property taxes

D. The process of assessing market value

Answer: A

Amortization refers to the process of paying off a loan over time through regular payments.

17. What is the primary purpose of a "debt service coverage ratio" (DSCR)?

A. To measure a property's income relative to its debt

B. To measure a property's market value

C. To measure a property's depreciation

D. To measure a property's tax liability

Answer: A

The primary purpose of a Debt Service Coverage Ratio (DSCR) is to measure a property's income relative to its debt obligations.

18. What does "gross rent multiplier" (GRM) help to determine?

A. The property's market value based on its rental income

B. The property's tax liability

C. The property's operating expenses

D. The property's mortgage payments

Answer: A

The Gross Rent Multiplier (GRM) helps to determine the property's market value based on its rental income.

19. What is "yield" in the context of real estate investment?

A. The annual return on an investment

B. The monthly rent income

C. The property's market value

D. The property's tax liability

Answer: A

Yield refers to the annual return on a real estate investment, usually expressed as a percentage of the property's value.

20. What is a "balloon payment" in a mortgage?

A. A large final payment to pay off the loan

B. A monthly mortgage payment

C. An initial down payment

D. A payment to cover property taxes

Answer: A

A balloon payment is a large final payment made at the end of a mortgage term to pay off the remaining balance.

21. What does "underwriting" refer to in real estate financing?

A. The process of evaluating the risk of a loan

B. The process of property valuation

C. The process of securing a mortgage

D. The process of property inspection

Answer: A

Underwriting refers to the process of evaluating the risk associated with granting a loan.

➡ 22. What is "leverage" in real estate investment?

A. Using borrowed funds to finance an investment

B. Increasing the property's market value

C. Reducing the property's operating expenses

D. Increasing the property's rental income

Answer: A

Leverage refers to the use of borrowed funds to finance a real estate investment.

➡ 23. What is "absorption rate" in real estate?

A. The rate at which properties are sold in a specific market

B. The rate at which properties appreciate in value

C. The rate at which properties are rented

D. The rate at which properties are foreclosed

Answer: A

Absorption rate is the rate at which available properties are sold in a specific market during a given time period.

➡ 24. What is a "seller's market"?

A. A market where supply exceeds demand

B. A market where demand exceeds supply

C. A market with stable prices

D. A market with declining prices

Answer: B

A seller's market is a market condition where demand exceeds supply, often leading to higher property prices.

25. What does "loan origination fee" refer to?

A. A fee for early repayment of a loan

B. A fee charged by a lender for processing a new loan

C. A fee for property inspection

D. A fee for property valuation

Answer: B

A loan origination fee is a fee charged by a lender for processing a new loan application.

26. What is the primary purpose of a "Comparative Market Analysis" (CMA)?

A. To determine the property's tax liability

B. To evaluate the property's insurance needs

C. To estimate the property's market value

D. To assess the property's structural integrity

Answer: C

The primary purpose of a Comparative Market Analysis (CMA) is to estimate the market value of a property by comparing it to similar properties that have recently sold or are currently on the market.

27. What does "cap rate" stand for?

A. Capital appreciation rate

B. Capitalization rate

C. Capital asset rate

D. Capital allocation rate

Answer: B

Cap rate stands for Capitalization Rate, which is used to calculate the value of income-generating properties.

28. What is "due diligence" in real estate?

A. The process of inspecting and verifying all aspects of a property before purchase

B. The process of securing a mortgage

C. The process of property valuation

D. The process of property renovation

Answer: A

Due diligence refers to the comprehensive appraisal of a property to confirm all facts, such as reviewing all financial records, plus anything else deemed material.

29. What is a "contingency" in a real estate contract?

A. A binding clause

B. A non-binding clause

C. A clause that makes the contract subject to certain conditions

D. A clause that outlines the penalties for contract violation

Answer: C

A contingency is a clause in a real estate contract that makes the contract subject to certain conditions that must be met by either the buyer or the seller.

30. What is "LTV" an acronym for?

A. Loan To Vendor
B. Loan To Value
C. Long-Term Valuation
D. Lease To Vendor

Answer: B

LTV stands for Loan To Value, which is a ratio used by lenders to calculate the risk of a loan.

31. What is "escrow"?

A. A type of mortgage
B. A legal arrangement where a third party temporarily holds funds or property
C. A type of property valuation
D. A type of property insurance

Answer: B

Escrow is a legal arrangement in which a third party holds funds or property until the conditions of a contract are met.

32. What does "NOI" stand for in real estate?

A. Net Operating Income
B. No Official Information
C. Net Official Interest
D. None Of the Interest

Answer: A

NOI stands for Net Operating Income, which is calculated as all revenue from the property minus all reasonably necessary operating expenses.

➡ 33. What is "appraisal"?

   A. The act of inspecting a property
   B. The act of determining the market value of a property
   C. The act of selling a property
   D. The act of buying a property

Answer: B

Appraisal is the act of determining the market value of a property, often conducted by a licensed appraiser.

➡ 34. What is "cash flow" in real estate?

   A. The total amount of money being transferred into and out of a business
   B. The total amount of money being invested
   C. The total amount of money being borrowed
   D. The total amount of money being taxed

Answer: A

Cash flow refers to the total amount of money being transferred into and out of a business, in this case, a property.

➡ 35. What is "common area maintenance" (CAM)?

   A. Maintenance of private property areas
   B. Maintenance of public property areas
   C. Maintenance of areas that are commonly used in a multi-tenant property
   D. Maintenance of all areas in a single-tenant property

Answer: C

Common Area Maintenance (CAM) is the maintenance of areas that are used by multiple tenants in a multi-tenant property.

36. What is the Debt-to-Income ratio primarily used for?

A. To assess property value
B. To evaluate loan eligibility
C. To calculate property taxes
D. To determine rent prices

Answer: B

The Debt-to-Income ratio is primarily used to evaluate a borrower's loan eligibility by comparing their debt payments to their income.

37. What does the term "amortization" refer to?

A. The process of increasing property value
B. The process of paying off a loan over time
C. The process of transferring property ownership
D. The process of calculating property taxes

Answer: B

Amortization refers to the process of paying off a loan over time through regular payments.

38. What is the primary focus of a "cost approach" in property valuation?

A. Comparable sales
B. Cost to rebuild the property
C. Income generated by the property
D. Current market trends

Answer: B

The cost approach focuses on the cost to rebuild the property as a method of valuation.

➟39. What does "LTV" stand for in mortgage financing?

A. Loan To Vendor
B. Loan To Value
C. Long Term Viability
D. Lease To Value

Answer: B

LTV stands for Loan To Value, which is the ratio of a loan to the value of the property.

➟40. What is the primary purpose of a "cap rate"?

A. To limit the amount of a loan
B. To evaluate the profitability of an investment property
C. To assess property taxes
D. To determine the interest rate of a loan

Answer: B

The primary purpose of a cap rate is to evaluate the profitability of an investment property.

➟41. What does "escrow" commonly refer to in real estate transactions?

A. A type of mortgage
B. A neutral third party holding funds
C. A property valuation method
D. A legal contract

Answer: B

Escrow commonly refers to a neutral third party holding funds or documents until the completion of a transaction.

➟42. What is "equity" in terms of real estate?

A. The market value of a property

B. The difference between the property's value and the mortgage owed

C. The annual income generated by a property

D. The initial down payment on a property

Answer: B

Equity is the difference between the market value of a property and the amount owed on its mortgage.

➡43. What does a "balloon payment" refer to?

A. A small initial down payment

B. A large final payment at the end of a loan term

C. Monthly mortgage payments

D. Annual property taxes

Answer: B

A balloon payment refers to a large final payment due at the end of a loan term.

➡44. What is the "principal" in a mortgage?

A. The initial down payment

B. The total cost of the property

C. The amount borrowed that has to be repaid

D. The interest rate

Answer: C

The principal is the amount borrowed that has to be repaid, not including interest.

➡45. What does "underwriting" refer to in mortgage financing?

A. Assessing the risk and eligibility of a loan

B. Calculating property taxes

C. Determining the market value of a property

D. Setting the terms and conditions of a lease

Answer: A

Underwriting refers to the process of assessing the risk and eligibility of a loan.

46. What is the "gross rent multiplier" used for?

A. To determine the profitability of a rental property

B. To calculate property taxes

C. To assess loan eligibility

D. To evaluate the cost of property maintenance

Answer: A

The gross rent multiplier is used to determine the profitability of a rental property by comparing the property's price to its gross rental income.

47. What does "compounding" refer to in the context of a mortgage?

A. The process of adding unpaid interest to the principal balance

B. The process of paying off a loan in full

C. The process of transferring property ownership

D. The process of calculating property taxes

Answer: A

Compounding refers to the process of adding unpaid interest to the principal balance of a loan.

48. What is a "contingency" in a real estate contract?

A. A mandatory clause

B. A penalty for late payment

C. A condition that must be met for the contract to proceed

D. A fixed interest rate

Answer: C

A contingency is a condition that must be met for the real estate contract to proceed.

➡49. What is "negative gearing" in real estate investment?

A. When the rental income covers all expenses

B. When the rental income is less than the expenses

C. When a property is sold at a profit

D. When a property is sold at a loss

Answer: B

Negative gearing occurs when the rental income generated by a property is less than the expenses, often leading to tax benefits.

➡50. What does "due diligence" refer to in real estate transactions?

A. The process of verifying all aspects of a deal

B. The initial down payment on a property

C. The final payment to close a deal

D. The process of property valuation

Answer: A

Due diligence refers to the process of thoroughly verifying all aspects of a real estate deal before proceeding.

Financing

Financing is the backbone of the real estate industry. Whether you're a first-time homebuyer, a seasoned investor, or a real estate professional, understanding the various financing options and processes is crucial. This chapter delves deep into the world of real estate financing, offering insights into loan types, the mortgage process, interest rates, and much more.

- Types of Financing

Conventional Loans

Conventional loans are the most common type of mortgage loans, offered by private lenders like banks and mortgage companies. They can be either conforming or non-conforming, depending on whether they meet the criteria set by Fannie Mae and Freddie Mac.

Fixed-Rate vs. Adjustable-Rate

Fixed-rate mortgages offer a constant interest rate and monthly payments over the life of the loan. Adjustable-rate mortgages (ARMs) have interest rates that may change periodically.

Government-Backed Loans

FHA Loans

Federal Housing Administration (FHA) loans are designed for low-to-moderate-income borrowers. They require lower minimum down payments and credit scores than many conventional loans.

VA Loans

VA loans are available to veterans, active-duty service members, and some members of the National Guard and Reserves. They offer benefits like no down payment and no private mortgage insurance (PMI).

USDA Loans

These are loans aimed at rural property buyers and are backed by the United States Department of Agriculture.

Alternative Financing Options

Bridge Loans

These are short-term loans that help you transition from one property to another.

Hard Money Loans

These are asset-based loans with higher interest rates and are typically used for investment properties.

Seller Financing

In some cases, the seller may agree to finance the property for you, eliminating the need for a traditional mortgage.

- The Mortgage Process: Step-by-Step

Pre-Approval and Pre-Qualification

Pre-approval is a more in-depth process than pre-qualification and involves submitting a mortgage application, along with documentation to verify your income, assets, and debts.

Loan Application

The loan application is a detailed form that gathers information about you and the property you're looking to buy.

Loan Estimate and Closing Disclosure

After your application, you'll receive a Loan Estimate form that outlines the terms of the loan and estimates of your closing costs.

Underwriting

The underwriter will assess your financial stability and the value of the property you're buying.

Appraisal

An appraisal will be conducted to determine the fair market value of the property.

Closing

This is the final step where all parties sign the necessary documents, and the loan is disbursed.

- Financial Metrics and Ratios

Loan-to-Value Ratio (LTV)

The LTV ratio is a measure used by lenders to assess risk, calculated by dividing the loan amount by the property's appraised value.

Debt-to-Income Ratio (DTI)

This ratio compares your monthly debt payments to your monthly gross income.

Credit Score

Your credit score plays a significant role in determining your eligibility for a loan.

- Costs and Fees

Down Payment

The down payment is usually a percentage of the property's price.

Closing Costs

These are fees paid at the closing of a real estate transaction, and they can include loan origination fees, appraisal fees, and attorney fees.

Points and Fees

Points are prepaid interest that can lower your mortgage's interest rate. Fees could include application fees, inspection fees, and more.

- Risks and Safeguards

Interest Rate Risks

Interest rates can be volatile, influenced by economic conditions and Federal Reserve policies.

Prepayment Penalties

Some loans may have penalties for paying them off early.

Foreclosure

If you default on your mortgage payments, the lender could foreclose on your property.

Mortgage Insurance

If your down payment is less than 20%, you may have to pay mortgage insurance.

- Conclusion

Understanding the complexities of real estate financing is crucial for anyone involved in a property transaction. This chapter has aimed to be a comprehensive guide, covering everything from loan types and the mortgage process to financial metrics and potential risks. With this knowledge, you are better equipped to navigate the complex landscape of real estate financing, making informed decisions that align with your financial goals.

Mock Exam Financing

1. What is the primary advantage of a 15-year mortgage over a 30-year mortgage?

   A. Lower interest rates
   B. Higher loan amounts
   C. Smaller monthly payments
   D. Longer amortization period

Answer: A

A 15-year mortgage typically comes with lower interest rates compared to a 30-year mortgage.

2. What is a balloon mortgage?

   A. A mortgage with fluctuating interest rates
   B. A mortgage with a large payment due at the end
   C. A mortgage with no down payment
   D. A mortgage with no interest

Answer: B

A balloon mortgage requires a large lump-sum payment at the end of the loan term.

3. What is the main purpose of a home equity loan?

   A. To purchase a new home
   B. To refinance an existing mortgage
   C. To borrow against the equity built in a home
   D. To finance home repairs

Answer: C

A home equity loan allows you to borrow against the equity you've built up in your home.

4. What is a reverse mortgage?

A. A loan for first-time homebuyers

B. A loan that pays the borrower monthly payments

C. A loan for investment properties

D. A loan for commercial properties

Answer: B

A reverse mortgage pays the borrower monthly payments based on their home equity.

5. What is a jumbo loan?

A. A loan below the conforming loan limits

B. A loan above the conforming loan limits

C. A loan for commercial properties

D. A loan for agricultural properties

Answer: B

A jumbo loan is a mortgage that exceeds the conforming loan limits set by federal agencies.

6. What does LTV stand for in mortgage financing?

A. Loan To Value

B. Long-Term Verification

C. Loan To Vendor

D. Long-Term Viability

Answer: A

LTV stands for Loan To Value, which is the ratio of a loan to the value of the property.

➟ 7. What is the primary purpose of mortgage insurance?

  A. To protect the lender
  B. To protect the borrower
  C. To lower interest rates
  D. To increase the loan amount

Answer: A

Mortgage insurance is designed to protect the lender in case the borrower defaults on the loan.

➟ 8. What is an adjustable-rate mortgage (ARM)?

  A. A mortgage with a fixed interest rate
  B. A mortgage with an interest rate that can change
  C. A mortgage with no interest
  D. A mortgage with a balloon payment

Answer: B

An adjustable-rate mortgage has an interest rate that can change periodically based on changes in a corresponding financial index.

➟ 9. What is a VA loan?

  A. A loan for veterans
  B. A loan for vacation homes
  C. A loan for very affluent individuals
  D. A loan for agricultural properties

Answer: A

A VA loan is a mortgage loan in the United States guaranteed by the United States Department of Veterans Affairs.

10. What is a debt-to-income ratio?

A. The ratio of monthly debt payments to monthly income
B. The ratio of loan amount to property value
C. The ratio of interest rate to loan amount
D. The ratio of down payment to loan amount

Answer: A

The debt-to-income ratio is the percentage of a consumer's monthly gross income that goes toward paying debts.

11. What is the primary advantage of a fixed-rate mortgage?

A. Lower initial payments
B. Interest rate changes over time
C. Interest rate remains the same
D. No down payment required

Answer: C

The primary advantage of a fixed-rate mortgage is that the interest rate remains the same throughout the loan term.

12. What does APR stand for?

A. Annual Property Rate
B. Annual Percentage Rate
C. Approved Payment Rate
D. Average Price Rate

Answer: B

APR stands for Annual Percentage Rate, which includes the interest rate and other loan costs.

13. What is a balloon mortgage?

A. A mortgage with no interest
B. A mortgage with fluctuating interest rates
C. A mortgage with a large payment at the end
D. A mortgage with small initial payments

Answer: C

A balloon mortgage requires a large lump-sum payment at the end of the loan term.

14. What is a home equity loan?

A. A loan for home repairs
B. A loan based on the home's value
C. A loan for first-time homebuyers
D. A loan for vacation homes

Answer: B

A home equity loan is a type of loan where the borrower uses the equity of his or her home as collateral.

15. What is a subprime mortgage?

A. A mortgage for prime properties
B. A mortgage with below-average interest rates
C. A mortgage for borrowers with poor credit
D. A mortgage for investment properties

Answer: C

A subprime mortgage is designed for borrowers with poor credit history.

➡ 16. What is refinancing?

    A. Buying a second home

    B. Replacing an existing loan with a new one

    C. Changing the terms of your mortgage

    D. Paying off a mortgage early

Answer: B

Refinancing involves replacing an existing loan with a new one, usually to get a lower interest rate.

➡ 17. What is a reverse mortgage?

    A. A mortgage for young people

    B. A mortgage that pays the borrower

    C. A mortgage for commercial properties

    D. A mortgage with reversed interest rates

Answer: B

A reverse mortgage is a loan where the lender pays the borrower, usually based on home equity.

➡ 18. What is a jumbo loan?

    A. A small mortgage

    B. A mortgage larger than government-set limits

    C. A mortgage for multiple properties

    D. A mortgage for mobile homes

Answer: B

A jumbo loan is a mortgage that exceeds the conforming loan limits set by government-sponsored entities.

19. What is underwriting?

A. The process of verifying loan information
B. The process of selling a mortgage
C. The process of setting interest rates
D. The process of paying off a mortgage

Answer: A

Underwriting is the process of evaluating the risk of insuring a home loan.

20. What is a conforming loan?

A. A loan that meets government guidelines
B. A loan for investment properties
C. A loan that adjusts over time
D. A loan for non-residential properties

Answer: A

A conforming loan is a mortgage that meets the guidelines set by government-sponsored entities.

21. What is the loan-to-value ratio?

A. The ratio of loan amount to property value
B. The ratio of interest to principal
C. The ratio of down payment to loan amount
D. The ratio of monthly payments to income

Answer: A

The loan-to-value ratio is the ratio of the loan amount to the appraised value of the property.

➟22. What is PMI?

A. Property Management Insurance
B. Private Mortgage Insurance
C. Public Mortgage Interest
D. Property Maintenance Index

Answer: B

PMI stands for Private Mortgage Insurance, which protects the lender in case of default.

➟23. What is an amortization schedule?

A. A schedule for property visits
B. A schedule of loan payments
C. A schedule for interest rate changes
D. A schedule for property taxes

Answer: B

An amortization schedule outlines the loan payments over time, showing principal and interest amounts.

➟24. What is a pre-approval letter?

A. A letter stating you have sold your home
B. A letter stating you are approved for a specific loan amount
C. A letter stating your credit score
D. A letter stating your home's appraisal value

Answer: B

A pre-approval letter indicates that you have been approved for a specific loan amount based on your financial standing.

➡ 25. What is an escrow account used for?

A. To hold the down payment
B. To hold funds for property taxes and insurance
C. To hold the loan amount
D. To hold funds for home repairs

Answer: B

An escrow account is used to hold funds for property taxes and insurance, which are paid periodically.

I apologize for the oversight. Here are the replacement questions for 26 and 29:

➡ 26. What is the primary purpose of a balloon mortgage?

A. To offer lower initial payments
B. To offer higher initial payments
C. To offer a fixed interest rate
D. To offer an adjustable interest rate

Answer: A

The primary purpose of a balloon mortgage is to offer lower initial payments, with a large sum due at the end of the loan term.

➡ 27. What is a bridge loan?

A. A loan for building bridges
B. A short-term loan to cover the gap between buying and selling homes
C. A loan for waterfront properties
D. A loan for commercial properties

Answer: B

A bridge loan is a short-term loan that helps cover the gap between the sale of an old home and the purchase of a new one.

➟28. What is a credit score?

A. A measure of property value

B. A measure of loan eligibility

C. A measure of financial responsibility

D. A measure of income

Answer: C

A credit score is a numerical representation of your financial responsibility, used by lenders to assess risk.

➟29. What is the main advantage of a fixed-rate mortgage?

A. Lower initial payments

B. Interest rate changes over time

C. Interest rate remains the same throughout the loan term

D. No down payment required

Answer: C

The main advantage of a fixed-rate mortgage is that the interest rate remains the same throughout the loan term, providing predictability in payments.

➟30. What is a down payment?

A. An initial payment to secure a loan

B. A payment made at the end of the loan term

C. A payment made to the real estate agent

D. A payment made to the insurance company

Answer: A

A down payment is an initial lump-sum payment made when purchasing a property, usually as a percentage of the property's price.

⇒31. What is the primary function of the Federal Reserve in relation to mortgage rates?

   A. Directly setting mortgage rates
   B. Influencing mortgage rates through monetary policy
   C. Offering mortgage loans to consumers
   D. Regulating the stock market

Answer: B

The Federal Reserve influences mortgage rates through its monetary policy, but it does not directly set them.

⇒32. What is the primary purpose of a "balloon payment" in a mortgage?

   A. To reduce the monthly payment
   B. To extend the loan term
   C. To pay off the loan early
   D. To adjust the interest rate

Answer: A

A balloon payment is a large, lump-sum payment made at the end of a loan term to pay off the remaining balance. It is primarily used to reduce the monthly payment over the term of the loan.

⇒33. What is the effect of a higher cap rate on a property's value?

   A. Increases the value
   B. Decreases the value

C. No effect on the value

D. Makes the value volatile

Answer: B

A higher capitalization rate (cap rate) generally indicates a higher perceived risk of the investment, which in turn decreases the property's value.

34. What does PITI stand for?

A. Principal, Interest, Taxes, Insurance

B. Payment, Interest, Taxes, Insurance

C. Principal, Income, Taxes, Insurance

D. Payment, Income, Taxes, Insurance

Answer: A

PITI stands for Principal, Interest, Taxes, and Insurance.

35. What does the term "underwriting" refer to in the context of mortgages?

A. The process of evaluating a borrower's creditworthiness

B. The process of setting interest rates

C. The process of selling a mortgage to another lender

D. The process of paying off a mortgage early

Answer: A

Underwriting refers to the process of evaluating a borrower's creditworthiness to determine the risk involved in granting a loan.

36. What is a prepayment penalty?

A. A fee for making extra payments on your mortgage

B. A fee for not making payments on time

C. A fee for refinancing your mortgage

D. A fee for paying off your mortgage early

Answer: D

A prepayment penalty is a fee that may be charged if you pay off your mortgage before the term is up.

37. What is a "jumbo loan"?

A. A loan that is smaller than the limits set by Fannie Mae and Freddie Mac

B. A loan that is larger than the limits set by Fannie Mae and Freddie Mac

C. A loan with a fixed interest rate

D. A loan with an adjustable interest rate

Answer: B

A jumbo loan is a loan that exceeds the conforming loan limits set by Fannie Mae and Freddie Mac.

38. What is the "debt-to-income ratio"?

A. The ratio of a borrower's total debt to their total income

B. The ratio of a borrower's mortgage debt to their total income

C. The ratio of a borrower's mortgage debt to the property value

D. The ratio of a borrower's total debt to the property value

Answer: A

The debt-to-income ratio is the ratio of a borrower's total debt to their total income, used to assess their ability to manage payments.

39. What is an escrow account primarily used for?

A. Paying off the mortgage

B. Paying property taxes and insurance

C. Paying the real estate agent's commission

D. Paying the down payment

Answer: B

An escrow account is primarily used for paying property taxes and insurance.

40. What is the main disadvantage of an adjustable-rate mortgage (ARM)?

A. Lower initial payments

B. Interest rate can increase over time

C. Fixed interest rate

D. No down payment required

Answer: B

The main disadvantage of an adjustable-rate mortgage is that the interest rate can increase over time, leading to higher payments.

41. What is a pre-qualification in mortgage terms?

A. A binding agreement between you and the lender

B. An estimate of how much you can afford to borrow

C. A guarantee of a loan

D. A finalized loan approval

Answer: B

Pre-qualification is an initial evaluation of your creditworthiness to give you an estimate of the loan amount you might qualify for.

42. What is the primary benefit of a fixed-rate mortgage?

A. Lower interest rates

B. Flexibility in payments

C. Interest rate remains constant

D. No down payment required

Answer: C

The primary benefit of a fixed-rate mortgage is that the interest rate remains constant throughout the loan term.

➡43. What is the primary role of Fannie Mae in the mortgage industry?

A. To provide home insurance

B. To act as a secondary mortgage market

C. To set federal funds rate

D. To issue mortgage-backed securities

Answer: B

Fannie Mae acts as a secondary mortgage market, buying and selling mortgages to free up funds for lenders.

➡44. What is the main advantage of a 15-year mortgage over a 30-year mortgage?

A. Lower interest rates

B. Smaller monthly payments

C. No down payment required

D. No closing costs

Answer: A

Generally, 15-year mortgages have lower interest rates compared to 30-year mortgages.

➡45. What is a home equity loan?

A. A loan for new home buyers

B. A loan based on the home's current market value

C. A loan that uses your home as collateral

D. A loan for home repairs

Answer: C

A home equity loan is a type of loan that uses your home as collateral and is often used to finance large expenses.

➡46. What is refinancing?

A. Taking a second mortgage on the property

B. Replacing an existing loan with a new one

C. Changing the terms of your existing loan

D. Paying off the mortgage early

Answer: B

Refinancing is the process of replacing an existing loan with a new one, often with better terms or lower interest rates.

➡47. What is an amortization schedule?

A. A list of all property assets

B. A timetable for paying off a loan

C. A schedule for home repairs

D. A list of all monthly expenses

Answer: B

An amortization schedule is a timetable that shows the breakdown of each payment into principal and interest and the remaining loan balance.

➡48. What is a reverse mortgage?

A. A mortgage for commercial properties

B. A mortgage that pays the borrower

C. A mortgage for first-time homebuyers

D. A mortgage with a variable interest rate

Answer: B

A reverse mortgage is a loan where the lender pays the borrower, often used by older homeowners to convert home equity into cash.

➟49. What is a jumbo loan?

A. A small, short-term loan

B. A loan that exceeds conforming loan limits

C. A loan for commercial properties

D. A loan with a high down payment

Answer: B

A jumbo loan is a mortgage that exceeds the conforming loan limits set by federal agencies and is not eligible for purchase, guarantee, or securitization by Fannie Mae or Freddie Mac.

➟50. What is the main purpose of a down payment?

A. To pay off the loan early

B. To lower the monthly payment

C. To secure the loan

D. To cover closing costs

Answer: C

The main purpose of a down payment is to secure the loan and reduce the lender's risk.

Transfer of Property

The transfer of property is not just a transaction; it's a complex legal process that requires meticulous attention to detail. Whether you're a buyer, a seller, or an agent, understanding the intricacies of property transfer is crucial. This chapter aims to serve as an exhaustive guide, covering everything from the types of property transfers to the legal instruments involved and the role of various professionals in the process.

- Types of Property Transfers

Voluntary vs. Involuntary

Voluntary Transfers

Sale: The most common form of voluntary transfer, usually facilitated by a real estate agent.
Gift: Transfer without any monetary exchange, often among family members.
Trust: Property can be transferred into a trust for tax benefits or estate planning.

Legal Aspects: Voluntary transfers usually require a written agreement and may involve complex contracts, especially when large assets are involved.

Involuntary Transfers

Foreclosure: When a property owner defaults on their mortgage payments.
Eminent Domain: The government can seize private property for public use.
Adverse Possession: Rare but possible, where someone gains property rights through unauthorized occupation.

Legal Aspects: Involuntary transfers often involve court proceedings and can be contested by the original owner under certain conditions.

By Sale

Steps Involved:

Listing the Property: Involves market analysis to set the right price.

Marketing: Various platforms are used to advertise the property.

Offer and Acceptance: Legal aspects of the offer, earnest money, and contingencies.

Due Diligence: Includes property inspection, title search, and securing financing.

Closing: Final steps, including escrow and legal paperwork.

By Inheritance or Gift

Wills and Probate: Legal processes involved in transferring property posthumously.

Gift Deeds: Legal requirements and tax implications.

- Legal Instruments in Property Transfer

Deed

Types of Deeds

General Warranty Deed: Offers the highest level of protection to the buyer, guaranteeing a clear title.

Special Warranty Deed: Limited to the time the seller owned the property.

Quitclaim Deed: Transfers any ownership the seller has, without any warranties.

Components of a Deed

Grantor and Grantee: Parties involved.

Legal Description: Detailed description of the property.

Consideration: The value exchanged.

Signatures: Both parties must sign, and the deed must be notarized.

Title

Title Search: Conducted to ensure the title is clear of any liens or encumbrances.
Title Insurance: Protects against future title disputes.

Bill of Sale

What it Covers: Lists all personal property included in the sale, like appliances and furniture.
Legal Requirements: Must be signed and may need to be notarized depending on the jurisdiction.

- The Role of Escrow

Opening an Escrow Account: How it's done and who chooses the escrow agent.
Escrow Instructions: Detailed instructions that the escrow agent must follow.
Closing Escrow: Final steps that include disbursement of funds and recording of deeds.

- Taxes and Fees

Transfer Taxes: Vary by state and sometimes by county.
Recording Fees: Costs for legally recording the new deed.
Other Costs: May include notary fees, title search fees, and more.

- Legal Requirements

Legal Capacity: Both parties must be of legal age and sound mind.
Written Contract: Real estate transactions must be in writing to be legally enforceable.
Consideration: This can be money, goods, or a promise to perform services.

- Closing Process

Final Walkthrough: Usually occurs 24 hours before closing.

Settlement Statement: A detailed list of all costs involved.

Signing of Documents: Includes the deed, mortgage papers if applicable, and the bill of sale.

Disbursement of Funds: The buyer's and seller's accounts are settled.

Recording the Deed: The deed is filed with the local county recorder's office.

Possession: The keys are handed over, and the new owner takes possession.

- Conclusion

The transfer of property is a multifaceted process that involves various steps, each with its own set of legal requirements and implications. Whether you're a first-time homebuyer or a seasoned real estate investor, understanding these elements is crucial for a smooth transaction. This chapter serves as a comprehensive guide, aiming to arm you with the knowledge you need to navigate the complexities of property transfers successfully.

Mock Exam Transfer of Property

➡1. What is the most common form of voluntary property transfer?

   A. Foreclosure
   B. Sale
   C. Eminent Domain
   D. Adverse Possession

Answer: B

Sale is the most common form of voluntary property transfer, usually facilitated by a real estate agent.

➡2. Which deed offers the highest level of protection to the buyer?

   A. Quitclaim Deed
   B. Special Warranty Deed
   C. General Warranty Deed
   D. None of the above

Answer: C

A General Warranty Deed offers the highest level of protection to the buyer, guaranteeing a clear title.

➡3. What is the purpose of a title search?

   A. To find the property's market value
   B. To ensure the title is clear of any liens or encumbrances
   C. To inspect the property
   D. To secure financing

Answer: B

A title search is conducted to ensure the title is clear of any liens or encumbrances.

➛4. What does a Bill of Sale cover?

   A. Personal property included in the sale

   B. The property's legal description

   C. The property's market value

   D. The property's zoning classification

Answer: A

A Bill of Sale lists all personal property included in the sale, like appliances and furniture.

➛5. What is the role of an escrow agent?

   A. To conduct a property inspection

   B. To follow detailed escrow instructions

   C. To set the property price

   D. To market the property

Answer: B

The role of an escrow agent is to follow detailed escrow instructions.

➛6. What is the final step in the closing process?

   A. Final walkthrough

   B. Signing of documents

   C. Disbursement of funds

   D. Possession

Answer: D

The final step in the closing process is possession, where the keys are handed over, and the new owner takes possession.

7. What is the legal process involved in transferring property posthumously?

A. Title search
B. Wills and Probate
C. Escrow
D. Due diligence

answer: B
Wills and Probate are the legal processes involved in transferring property posthumously.

8. What is a gift deed?

A. A deed used in property sales
B. A deed used in foreclosures
C. A deed used in property gifts
D. A deed used in auctions

Answer: C
A gift deed is used in property gifts, often among family members.

9. What is eminent domain?

A. A type of deed
B. A type of voluntary transfer
C. The government's right to seize private property for public use
D. A type of mortgage

Answer: C
Eminent domain is the government's right to seize private property for public use.

10. What is adverse possession?

A. A type of voluntary transfer

B. A type of involuntary transfer

C. A type of mortgage

D. A type of deed

Answer: B

Adverse possession is a type of involuntary transfer where someone gains property rights through unauthorized occupation.

11. What is the primary purpose of a deed?

A. To transfer title

B. To secure a loan

C. To outline property boundaries

D. To list property amenities

Answer:

A. The primary purpose of a deed is to transfer title from the grantor to the grantee.

12. What is the difference between a quitclaim deed and a warranty deed?

A. A quitclaim deed offers no warranties

B. A warranty deed is only used in foreclosures

C. A quitclaim deed transfers only the grantor's interest

D. Both A and C

Answer: D.

A quitclaim deed offers no warranties and transfers only the grantor's interest in the property.

➡ 13. What does "chain of title" refer to?

A. A series of owners of a property
B. The length of a property's boundary
C. The number of liens on a property
D. The process of surveying a property

Answer: A.

The chain of title refers to the series of owners that a property has had over time.

➡ 14. What is "alienation" in the context of property?

A. The process of transferring property rights
B. The act of renting out a property
C. The act of taking someone's property unlawfully
D. The process of subdividing a property

Answer: A.

Alienation refers to the process of transferring property rights from one party to another.

➡ 15. What is a "grantee" in a deed?

A. The person transferring the property
B. The person receiving the property
C. The person who witnesses the deed
D. The person who notarizes the deed

Answer: B.

The grantee is the person receiving the property as specified in the deed.

➡ 16. What does "encumbrance" mean?

A. Free and clear ownership

B. A claim against a property

C. A type of property deed

D. A type of property insurance

Answer: B.

An encumbrance is a claim against a property that may restrict its transfer or use.

➡ 17. What is "adverse possession"?

A. Unlawful ownership of property

B. Gaining legal ownership through open and notorious possession

C. A type of property insurance

D. A type of property deed

Answer: B.

Adverse possession is the process of gaining legal ownership of a property through open, continuous, and notorious possession.

➡ 18. What is "escheat"?

A. A type of property tax

B. The reversion of property to the state when there are no heirs

C. A type of property insurance

D. A type of property deed

Answer: B.

Escheat is the reversion of property to the state when there are no legal heirs.

➡ 19. What is a "life estate"?

A. A property owned for a lifetime

B. A property that can only be sold after the owner's death

C. A property owned only for a specified number of years

D. A property that reverts to the state after the owner's death

Answer: A.

A life estate is a property interest that lasts for the lifetime of the holder.

➡20. What is "eminent domain"?

A. The right of the government to take private property for public use

B. The right of the owner to use the property as they see fit

C. The right of the state to tax property

D. The right of the owner to sell the property

Answer: A.

Eminent domain is the right of the government to take private property for public use, usually with compensation to the owner.

➡21. What is the role of a title company in a property transfer?

A. To provide financing

B. To ensure clear title

C. To conduct a property survey

D. To negotiate the sale price

Answer: B. To ensure clear title

The title company is responsible for conducting a title search to ensure that the title to the property is clear and can be transferred without any legal issues.

➡22. What is a "cloud on title"?

A. A type of property insurance

B. A pending legal claim against a property

C. A type of property deed

D. A property that is free and clear of any encumbrances

Answer: B. A pending legal claim against a property

A cloud on title refers to any condition that affects the clear title of a property, such as a lien or an unresolved legal issue.

➡ 23. What is "title insurance"?

A. Insurance against property damage

B. Insurance against title defects

C. Insurance against property theft

D. Insurance against property depreciation

Answer: B. Insurance against title defects

Title insurance protects against financial loss due to defects in the title, such as fraud or errors in the public record.

➡ 24. What is a "1031 exchange"?

A. A type of mortgage

B. A tax-deferred property exchange

C. A type of property insurance

D. A type of property deed

Answer: B. A tax-deferred property exchange

A 1031 exchange allows the owner to sell a property and reinvest the proceeds in a new property while deferring capital gains tax.

➡ 25. What is "right of first refusal"?

A. The right to purchase a property before it is offered to others

B. The right to refuse a property inspection

C. The right to refuse to pay property taxes

D. The right to refuse to sell a property

Answer: A. The right to purchase a property before it is offered to others
Right of first refusal gives a person or entity the opportunity to purchase a property before the owner offers it for sale to other parties.

26. What is "power of attorney"?

A. The power to sell a property

B. The power to make decisions on behalf of another

C. The power to mortgage a property

D. The power to lease a property

Answer: B. The power to make decisions on behalf of another
Power of attorney is a legal document that allows one person to act on behalf of another, including in property transactions.

27. What is "equity" in real estate?

A. The market value of a property

B. The difference between the property's value and the mortgage balance

C. The annual property tax

D. The monthly mortgage payment

Answer: B. The difference between the property's value and the mortgage balance
Equity is the difference between the market value of a property and the amount owed on any mortgages or liens against it.

28. What is a "balloon payment"?

A. A large final payment on a loan
B. A monthly mortgage payment
C. A property tax payment
D. A down payment on a property

Answer: A. A large final payment on a loan
A balloon payment is a large, lump-sum payment that is due at the end of a loan term.

29. What is "amortization"?

A. The process of increasing property value
B. The process of paying off a loan over time
C. The process of transferring property
D. The process of insuring a property

Answer: B. The process of paying off a loan over time
Amortization is the process of gradually reducing a loan balance through regular payments over a period of time.

30. What is "redlining"?

A. Drawing property boundaries
B. Discriminatory lending practices
C. A type of property survey
D. A type of property deed

Answer: B. Discriminatory lending practices
Redlining is an illegal practice where lenders refuse loans or insurance to people based on their race, ethnicity, or location.

31. What is the purpose of an "escrow account" in a property transaction?

A. To hold the down payment

B. To pay property taxes

C. To hold funds for future repairs

D. To pay the real estate agent's commission

Answer: A. To hold the down payment

An escrow account is used to hold the buyer's down payment until the property transaction is completed.

32. What does "chain of title" refer to?

A. A series of owners of a property

B. A type of property insurance

C. A type of property deed

D. A series of property inspections

Answer: A. A series of owners of a property

Chain of title refers to the sequence of historical transfers of title to a property.

33. What is a "quitclaim deed"?

A. Transfers property with no warranties

B. Transfers property with warranties

C. A deed used in foreclosures

D. A deed used in new constructions

Answer: A. Transfers property with no warranties

A quitclaim deed transfers ownership without any warranties or guarantees that the title is clear.

34. What is a "seller's disclosure"?

A. A document detailing the property's flaws

B. A document detailing the property's price

C. A document detailing the property's history

D. A document detailing the property's zoning

Answer: A. A document detailing the property's flaws

A seller's disclosure is a document where the seller lists known defects or issues with the property.

35. What is "eminent domain"?

A. The right of the government to take private property

B. The right of the owner to modify the property

C. The right of the tenant to buy the property

D. The right of the lender to foreclose on the property

Answer: A. The right of the government to take private property

Eminent domain is the power of the government to take private property for public use, usually with compensation.

36. What is "adverse possession"?

A. Illegal occupation of a property

B. Legal claim to a property after long-term occupation

C. A type of property insurance

D. A type of property deed

Answer: B. Legal claim to a property after long-term occupation

Adverse possession allows someone to gain legal ownership of a property after occupying it for a certain period, provided certain conditions are met.

37. What is a "real estate short sale"?

A. Selling a property for less than the mortgage owed

B. Selling a property quickly

C. Selling a property at auction

D. Selling a property for cash

Answer: A. Selling a property for less than the mortgage owed

A short sale occurs when a property is sold for less than the amount owed on the mortgage, usually with lender approval.

➡38. What is "condemnation"?

A. The act of publicly criticizing a property

B. The act of declaring a property unfit for use

C. The act of selling a property

D. The act of insuring a property

Answer: B. The act of declaring a property unfit for use

Condemnation is the legal process of declaring a property unfit for use, often leading to its seizure or destruction.

➡39. What is "due diligence" in real estate?

A. The process of inspecting a property before purchase

B. The process of appraising a property

C. The process of insuring a property

D. The process of transferring a property

Answer: A. The process of inspecting a property before purchase

Due diligence involves thoroughly investigating a property before purchase to identify any potential issues or liabilities.

➡40. What is "fair market value"?

A. The highest price a property can sell for

B. The lowest price a property can sell for

C. The price a property would sell for under normal conditions

D. The price a property would sell for at auction

Answer: C. The price a property would sell for under normal conditions

Fair market value is the price that a property would sell for on the open market, between a willing buyer and a willing seller.

➡ 41. What is the primary purpose of a "title search"?

A. To find the property's market value

B. To verify the legal ownership of the property

C. To assess the property's condition

D. To determine the property's zoning

Answer: B. To verify the legal ownership of the property

A title search is conducted to confirm the legal ownership of the property and discover any liens, encumbrances, or other issues with the title.

➡ 42. What is "equity" in terms of real estate?

A. The difference between the property's value and the mortgage owed

B. The initial down payment on a property

C. The interest rate on a mortgage

D. The property's appreciation over time

Answer: A. The difference between the property's value and the mortgage owed

Equity is the value of the property minus any debts or liens against it, such as a mortgage.

➡ 43. What is a "contingency" in a real estate contract?

A. A mandatory clause

B. An optional clause that must be met for the contract to proceed

C. A penalty for breaching the contract

D. A type of insurance policy

Answer: B. An optional clause that must be met for the contract to proceed

A contingency is a condition that must be fulfilled for the real estate contract to proceed, such as a successful home inspection.

➡ 44. What is "amortization"?

A. The process of increasing property value

B. The process of paying off a loan over time

C. The process of transferring property ownership

D. The process of appraising a property

Answer: B. The process of paying off a loan over time

Amortization refers to the gradual reduction of a loan balance through regular payments over time.

➡ 45. What is a "balloon mortgage"?

A. A mortgage with fluctuating interest rates

B. A mortgage that must be paid off in a short period

C. A mortgage with low initial payments

D. A mortgage with no down payment

Answer: B. A mortgage that must be paid off in a short period

A balloon mortgage requires a large lump sum payment at the end of the loan term, usually after a series of smaller payments.

➡ 46. What is "redlining"?

A. Drawing property boundaries

B. Discriminatory lending practices

C. Highlighting important clauses in a contract

D. Setting maximum property prices

Answer: B. Discriminatory lending practices

Redlining is an illegal practice where lenders discriminate based on geographic location, often targeting minority communities.

➡ 47. What is "appraisal"?

A. The act of inspecting a property

B. The act of determining a property's market value

C. The act of selling a property

D. The act of buying a property

Answer: B. The act of determining a property's market value

An appraisal is an evaluation to determine a property's market value, usually conducted by a certified appraiser.

➡ 48. What is "subletting"?

A. Renting out a property you own

B. Renting out a property you are renting

C. Buying a secondary property

D. Selling a rented property

Answer: B. Renting out a property you are renting

Subletting involves renting out a property (or part of it) that you are already renting from a landlord.

➡ 49. What is a "reverse mortgage"?

A. A mortgage for seniors to convert equity into cash

B. A mortgage with decreasing interest rates

C. A mortgage paid in reverse order

D. A mortgage for commercial properties

Answer: A. A mortgage for seniors to convert equity into cash

A reverse mortgage allows seniors to convert their home equity into cash, usually without monthly payments.

50. What is "staging" in real estate?

A. The process of legalizing a property sale

B. The process of decorating a property for sale

C. The process of surveying a property

D. The process of appraising a property

Answer: B. The process of decorating a property for sale

Staging involves decorating and arranging a property to make it more appealing to potential buyers.

Practice of Real Estate and Disclosures

The real estate industry is a complex field that involves various stakeholders, including buyers, sellers, agents, and financial institutions. One of the most critical aspects that often gets overlooked is the practice of disclosures. Disclosures are not just a legal formality; they are an ethical and legal obligation that can significantly impact the transaction process. This chapter aims to provide an in-depth understanding of the practice of real estate and the role of disclosures in it.

- The Scope of Real Estate Practice

Property Listing and Marketing

Real estate agents use multiple platforms, including MLS (Multiple Listing Service), social media, and traditional advertising methods like billboards and flyers, to list and market properties. The effectiveness of these platforms varies depending on the target audience and property type.

Property Valuation

Valuation is a critical aspect that involves various methods like the Sales Comparison Approach, Cost Approach, and Income Capitalization Approach. Each method has its pros and cons, and the choice often depends on the property type and market conditions.

Contract Negotiation

This involves not just haggling over the price but also negotiating the terms and conditions, contingencies, and other aspects of the contract. Both parties may involve legal advisors to ensure that the contract abides by state and federal laws.

Closing Transactions

The closing process involves multiple steps, including final walkthroughs, document verification, and the actual transfer of funds. Each of these steps is crucial and requires meticulous attention to detail.

Property Management

This includes not just maintenance but also tenant management, rent collection, and compliance with local and state regulations. Property managers often use software tools to streamline these processes.

Consultation

Real estate agents often provide consultation services, advising clients on market trends, investment opportunities, and renovation ideas that could increase property value.

- Importance of Disclosures

Protect the Buyer

Disclosures serve as a protective measure for buyers, offering them a clear understanding of the property's condition, which is crucial for making an informed decision.

Protect the Seller

By providing accurate disclosures, sellers can protect themselves from potential legal issues that may arise post-sale due to undisclosed property conditions.

Facilitate Transparency

Disclosures ensure that all parties are on the same page, reducing the likelihood of misunderstandings and disputes.

- Types of Disclosures

Material Facts

These are facts that could materially affect the property's value. For example, if the property has ever been the site of a crime, that's considered a material fact that could influence a buyer's decision.

Legal Disclosures

These include zoning laws, property lines, and any legal issues the property may have, such as pending litigation related to property boundaries.

Environmental Disclosures

These are especially important in older properties that may contain hazardous materials like asbestos or lead-based paint. Failure to disclose such information can lead to severe legal consequences.

Financial Disclosures

These include any liens on the property, past bankruptcies, or other financial issues that could affect the transaction.

- The Role of Agents in Disclosures

Real estate agents are often the mediators in the disclosure process. They are legally obligated to ensure that all disclosures are made accurately and in a timely manner. Agents use standard forms like the Seller's Disclosure form to facilitate this process.

- Legal Consequences of Inadequate Disclosures

Civil Penalties

Failure to disclose can result in hefty fines for both the seller and the agent. These fines can vary depending on the jurisdiction and the severity of the omission.

Legal Suits

Buyers have the right to sue both the seller and the agent for damages if they discover undisclosed issues with the property. This can result in costly legal battles and potential financial ruin for the seller and the agent.

License Revocation

For agents, the failure to disclose can result in disciplinary action from the real estate licensing board, including the revocation of their license.

- Best Practices for Disclosures

Documentation

Always document all disclosures. This documentation can serve as legal proof in case of any disputes.

Verification

It's not enough to take the seller's word for it. Agents should verify all information to the best of their ability before making a disclosure.

Timeliness

Disclosures should be made as early as possible in the transaction process. This not only helps the buyer but also protects the seller and the agent from potential legal issues.

- Conclusion

The practice of real estate is a complex field that requires a deep understanding of various aspects, from property valuation to legal obligations like disclosures. Disclosures are not just a legal formality but a critical aspect that can significantly impact the transaction process. By understanding the scope and importance of disclosures, you can navigate the complexities of the real estate industry more effectively.

Mock Exam Practice of Real Estate and Disclosures

1. What is the primary purpose of disclosures in real estate transactions?

A. To protect the buyer
B. To protect the seller
C. To facilitate transparency
D. All of the above

Answer: **D. All of the above**

Disclosures serve to protect both the buyer and the seller while also facilitating transparency in the transaction.

2. What is the MLS?

A. Mortgage Lending Service
B. Multiple Listing Service
C. Money Laundering Scheme
D. Municipal Land Survey

Answer: **B. Multiple Listing Service**

MLS stands for Multiple Listing Service, a platform used for listing and marketing properties.

3. What is the Sales Comparison Approach primarily used for?

A. Property Listing
B. Property Valuation
C. Contract Negotiation
D. Property Management

Answer: **B. Property Valuation**

The Sales Comparison Approach is mainly used for property valuation by comparing similar properties that have recently sold.

⇒4. Which of the following is NOT a type of disclosure?

A. Material Facts
B. Legal Disclosures
C. Environmental Disclosures
D. Aesthetic Disclosures

Answer: D. Aesthetic Disclosures
Aesthetic Disclosures are not a standard type of disclosure in real estate transactions.

⇒5. What can happen to a real estate agent who fails to make adequate disclosures?

A. Civil Penalties
B. Legal Suits
C. License Revocation
D. All of the above

Answer: D. All of the above
Failure to disclose can result in civil penalties, legal suits, and even license revocation for the real estate agent.

⇒6. What is the role of real estate agents in the disclosure process?

A. To verify all information
B. To document all disclosures
C. To make disclosures in a timely manner
D. All of the above

Answer: D. All of the above

Agents are obligated to verify, document, and make disclosures in a timely manner.

7. What is NOT a part of the closing transactions?

A. Final walkthroughs
B. Document verification
C. Property Valuation
D. Transfer of funds

Answer: C. Property Valuation

Property Valuation is not typically a part of the closing transactions but is done much earlier in the process.

8. What does property management NOT include?

A. Maintenance
B. Tenant management
C. Rent collection
D. Property listing

Answer: D. Property listing

Property listing is generally not a part of property management; it's more related to the sales aspect.

9. What is the primary purpose of the Seller's Disclosure form?

A. To list the property
B. To facilitate the disclosure process
C. To negotiate the contract
D. To close the transaction

Answer: B. To facilitate the disclosure process

The Seller's Disclosure form is used to facilitate the disclosure process by providing a standardized format.

10. What is NOT a method of property valuation?

A. Sales Comparison Approach
B. Cost Approach
C. Income Capitalization Approach
D. Random Guessing

Answer: D. Random Guessing
Random Guessing is not a professional method of property valuation.

11. What is the primary role of a buyer's agent?

A. Represent the seller
B. Represent the buyer
C. Represent both buyer and seller
D. None of the above

Answer: B. Represent the buyer
The primary role of a buyer's agent is to represent the interests of the buyer in a real estate transaction.

12. What does the term "dual agency" mean?

A. Two agents representing the buyer
B. One agent representing both buyer and seller
C. Two agents representing the seller
D. None of the above

Answer: B. One agent representing both buyer and seller

Dual agency refers to a situation where one agent represents both the buyer and the seller in a transaction.

➡13. What is a "contingency" in a real estate contract?

A. A binding clause
B. A non-binding clause
C. A conditional clause
D. An illegal clause

Answer: C. A conditional clause
A contingency is a conditional clause that must be met for the contract to be binding.

➡14. What is earnest money?

A. A loan from the bank
B. A gift from the seller to the buyer
C. A deposit made by the buyer
D. A tax imposed by the government

Answer: C. A deposit made by the buyer
Earnest money is a deposit made by the buyer to show good faith in a transaction.

➡15. What does "FSBO" stand for?

A. For Sale By Owner
B. For Sale By Operator
C. Fixed Sale By Order
D. Final Sale By Owner

Answer: A. For Sale By Owner

FSBO stands for For Sale By Owner, indicating that the property is being sold without a listing agent.

16. What is the main purpose of a title search?

A. To find the property's market value
B. To ensure the property is legally available for sale
C. To inspect the property's condition
D. To assess property taxes

Answer: B. To ensure the property is legally available for sale

A title search ensures that the property is legally available for sale and free of liens or other issues.

17. What is a "listing agreement"?

A. A contract between buyer and seller
B. A contract between seller and agent
C. A contract between buyer and agent
D. A contract between two agents

Answer: B. A contract between seller and agent

A listing agreement is a contract between the seller and the listing agent, outlining the terms of the property sale.

18. What is "escrow"?

A. A type of mortgage
B. A neutral third party in a transaction
C. A legal dispute
D. A type of property insurance

Answer: B. A neutral third party in a transaction

Escrow refers to a neutral third party that holds funds or documents until the transaction is completed.

19. What does "under contract" mean in a real estate context?

A. The property is listed for sale
B. An offer has been accepted, but the sale isn't final
C. The property has been sold
D. The property is off the market

Answer: B. An offer has been accepted, but the sale isn't final

"Under contract" means that an offer on the property has been accepted, but the sale has not yet been finalized.

20. What is a "puffing" statement?

A. A factual statement about the property
B. An exaggerated statement to promote the property
C. A misleading statement that is illegal
D. A statement made by the buyer

Answer: B. An exaggerated statement to promote the property

A "puffing" statement is an exaggerated claim made to promote the property, but it is not considered illegal.

21. What is the role of a transaction broker?

A. Represent only the seller
B. Represent only the buyer
C. Facilitate the transaction without representing either party
D. Represent both the buyer and the seller

Answer: C. Facilitate the transaction without representing either party

A transaction broker helps facilitate the real estate transaction but does not represent either the buyer or the seller.

➡ 22. What does "right of first refusal" mean?

A. The right to refuse any offer
B. The right to be the first to make an offer
C. The right to match any offer before the property is sold to someone else
D. The right to be the last to make an offer

Answer: C. The right to match any offer before the property is sold to someone else

The right of first refusal allows a party the opportunity to match any offer before the property is sold to another buyer.

➡ 23. What is a "pocket listing"?

A. A listing that is not publicly advertised
B. A listing that is only advertised online
C. A listing that is advertised in newspapers
D. A listing that is shared among agents

Answer: A. A listing that is not publicly advertised

A pocket listing is a property that an agent keeps "in their pocket" and does not list on the MLS or advertise publicly.

➡ 24. What is a "seller's market"?

A. A market with more buyers than sellers
B. A market with more sellers than buyers
C. A market with equal numbers of buyers and sellers
D. A market where only commercial properties are sold

Answer: A. A market with more buyers than sellers

A seller's market occurs when demand exceeds supply, giving sellers an advantage.

25. What is "redlining"?

A. A legal practice in real estate

B. An illegal discriminatory practice

C. A type of property insurance

D. A method of property valuation

Answer: B. An illegal discriminatory practice

Redlining is an illegal practice where services are denied to residents of certain areas based on their racial or ethnic composition.

26. What does "amortization" refer to?

A. The process of increasing property value

B. The process of paying off a loan over time

C. The process of transferring property ownership

D. The process of evaluating a property's condition

Answer: B. The process of paying off a loan over time

Amortization refers to the gradual repayment of a loan over a specified period.

27. What is "zoning"?

A. The process of dividing land into zones for specific uses

B. The process of evaluating a property's value

C. The process of transferring property

D. The process of obtaining a mortgage

Answer: A. The process of dividing land into zones for specific uses

Zoning involves dividing land into zones that dictate how the land can be used.

28. What is "curb appeal"?

A. The attractiveness of a property from the street
B. The interior design of a property
C. The legal aspects of a property
D. The cost of a property

Answer: A. The attractiveness of a property from the street

Curb appeal refers to how attractive the property appears from the outside or from the "curb."

29. What is "equity" in real estate?

A. The value of the property minus any loans
B. The total value of the property
C. The amount of the mortgage
D. The amount of rent charged

Answer: A. The value of the property minus any loans

Equity is the difference between the market value of the property and any outstanding loans or liens against it.

30. What is a "short sale"?

A. A quick sale of a property
B. A sale where the proceeds are less than the outstanding mortgage
C. A sale involving only cash
D. A sale involving a short-term lease

Answer: B. A sale where the proceeds are less than the outstanding mortgage

A short sale occurs when the sale price is less than the remaining balance on the mortgage, often due to financial hardship.

31. What is "dual agency"?

A. Representing both the buyer and the seller in a transaction

B. Representing only the buyer

C. Representing only the seller

D. Representing neither the buyer nor the seller

Answer: A. Representing both the buyer and the seller in a transaction

Dual agency occurs when a single agent represents both the buyer and the seller in a real estate transaction.

32. What is "title insurance"?

A. Insurance for property damage

B. Insurance for the mortgage

C. Insurance that protects against legal issues with the property title

D. Insurance for renters

Answer: C. Insurance that protects against legal issues with the property title

Title insurance protects against defects in the title, ensuring that the buyer has clear ownership of the property.

33. What is a "contingency" in a real estate contract?

A. A fixed term in the contract

B. A condition that must be met for the contract to proceed

C. An illegal clause

D. A non-negotiable clause

Answer: B. A condition that must be met for the contract to proceed

A contingency is a condition that must be fulfilled for the contract to move forward, such as a successful home inspection.

➥ 34. What is "escrow"?

A. A type of mortgage
B. A third-party account holding funds until conditions are met
C. A legal dispute
D. A type of property valuation

Answer: B. A third-party account holding funds until conditions are met

Escrow is an account where funds are held by a third party until certain conditions are met, such as the closing of a sale.

➥ 35. What does "FSBO" stand for?

A. For Sale By Owner
B. Fixed Sale By Offer
C. For Sale By Operator
D. Fixed Sale By Operator

Answer: A. For Sale By Owner

FSBO stands for "For Sale By Owner," indicating that the property is being sold directly by the owner without a listing agent.

➥ 36. What is "negative amortization"?

A. When the loan balance decreases
B. When the loan balance increases
C. When the property value increases
D. When the property value decreases

Answer: B. When the loan balance increases

Negative amortization occurs when the monthly payments are not enough to cover the interest, causing the loan balance to increase.

➡ 37. What is a "balloon mortgage"?

A. A mortgage with fluctuating interest rates
B. A mortgage with a large final payment
C. A mortgage with no down payment
D. A mortgage with a fixed interest rate

Answer: B. A mortgage with a large final payment

A balloon mortgage requires a large lump-sum payment at the end of the loan term.

➡ 38. What is "staging" in real estate?

A. Decorating a property to sell
B. Evaluating a property's value
C. Preparing legal documents
D. Conducting a home inspection

Answer: A. Decorating a property to sell

Staging involves decorating and arranging a property to make it more appealing to potential buyers.

➡ 39. What is a "pre-approval" in a mortgage process?

A. A final approval for a mortgage
B. A preliminary approval based on creditworthiness
C. A type of mortgage insurance
D. A type of property inspection

Answer: B. A preliminary approval based on creditworthiness

Pre-approval is an initial assessment that determines how much a buyer can afford to borrow based on their financial situation.

➡ 40. What is "leverage" in real estate?

A. Using borrowed funds for investment
B. The process of selling a property
C. The process of buying a property
D. The rate of return on a property

Answer: A. Using borrowed funds for investment

Leverage involves using borrowed capital for an investment and expecting the profits to be greater than the interest payable.

➡ 41. What is "equity" in real estate?

A. The market value of a property
B. The difference between the property's value and the mortgage balance
C. The initial down payment
D. The annual property tax

Answer: B. The difference between the property's value and the mortgage balance

Equity is the financial interest you have in your property, calculated as the property's current market value minus any remaining mortgage balance.

➡ 42. What is "redlining"?

A. A type of home inspection
B. Discriminatory practice in lending or insurance
C. A method of property valuation
D. A type of mortgage

Answer: B. Discriminatory practice in lending or insurance

Redlining is an illegal practice where services like loans or insurance are denied to people based on their geographic area, often targeting minority communities.

➡ 43. What is "appraisal"?

A. A legal document
B. An estimate of a property's value
C. A type of mortgage
D. A home inspection report

Answer: B. An estimate of a property's value

An appraisal is a professional assessment of a property's market value, usually conducted by a licensed appraiser.

➡ 44. What is "underwriting" in the context of a mortgage?

A. The process of verifying financial information
B. The process of home inspection
C. The act of transferring property title
D. The act of selling a property

Answer: A. The process of verifying financial information

Underwriting involves assessing the creditworthiness of the borrower and the value of the property to determine the risk of the loan.

➡ 45. What is a "closing cost"?

A. The cost of home inspection
B. The cost of property appraisal
C. Additional fees paid at the end of a real estate transaction
D. The initial down payment

Answer: C. Additional fees paid at the end of a real estate transaction

Closing costs are additional expenses, aside from the property price, that buyers and sellers incur at the end of a real estate transaction.

46. What is "PMI"?

A. Property Market Index

B. Private Mortgage Insurance

C. Property Management Institution

D. Public Mortgage Investment

Answer: B. Private Mortgage Insurance

PMI stands for Private Mortgage Insurance, which is usually required when the down payment is less than 20% of the property's value.

47. What is a "short sale"?

A. A quick sale of a property

B. Selling a property for less than the mortgage owed

C. A discounted property sale

D. Selling a property within a week

Answer: B. Selling a property for less than the mortgage owed

A short sale occurs when a property is sold for less than the amount owed on the mortgage, usually with lender approval.

48. What is "condominium ownership"?

A. Owning a single-family home

B. Owning an individual unit in a multi-unit building

C. Owning a rental property

D. Owning a commercial property

Answer: B. Owning an individual unit in a multi-unit building

In a condominium, you own an individual unit within a larger building or community, along with shared ownership of common areas.

49. What is "earnest money"?

A. The total cost of a property
B. A deposit showing the buyer's intent to purchase
C. The final payment in a mortgage
D. Money paid for a property appraisal

Answer: B. A deposit showing the buyer's intent to purchase

Earnest money is a deposit made to a seller indicating the buyer's intent to complete the purchase, typically refundable only under certain conditions.

50. What is "right of first refusal"?

A. The right to buy a property before others
B. The right to refuse a property inspection
C. The right to refuse mortgage terms
D. The right to sell a property before others

Answer: A. The right to buy a property before others

The right of first refusal allows a person the opportunity to buy a property before the owner sells it to another party.

Contracts

Contracts are not just legal documents; they are the backbone of all real estate transactions. They set the stage for the relationship between the buyer, seller, and any other parties involved. A well-drafted contract can be the difference between a smooth transaction and a legal nightmare. This chapter aims to provide an in-depth understanding of the various types of contracts you'll encounter, their legal prerequisites, and the intricacies of common clauses.

- Types of Contracts

Purchase Agreements

Also known as a Sale Contract, this is the cornerstone of any real estate transaction. It outlines not just the price and date of sale, but also any conditions that must be met beforehand, such as repairs or financing.

Subtypes of Purchase Agreements

As-Is Agreement: The property is sold in its current condition; no repairs will be made.
Conditional Sale Agreement: The sale is conditional upon certain criteria, such as the sale of the buyer's current home.

Lease Agreements

These are not just for residential properties; commercial real estate often involves complex lease agreements that can span several years and include various stipulations.

Types of Leases

Gross Lease: Tenant pays a flat rent; the landlord pays for all property charges.
Net Lease: Tenant pays a lower base rent plus property expenses.

Option Agreements

These are particularly useful for buyers who need time to secure financing or for investors who want to lock in a price for future purchase.

Types of Options

Lease Option: Combines a lease and a purchase option.
Straight Option: Buyer pays for the exclusive right to purchase within a certain time.

- Essential Elements of a Contract

Offer and Acceptance

The offer must be clear, and acceptance must be unconditional. Any counteroffers should be treated as new offers.

Consideration

This is not limited to money; it can also be a promise to perform a service, or even love and affection in some cases.

Legal Purpose

Contracts for illegal activities, such as selling a property for the purpose of conducting illegal activities, are null and void.

Competent Parties

Minors, intoxicated individuals, and mentally incapacitated persons cannot enter into contracts.

- Common Clauses

Contingency Clauses

These can range from financing contingencies to inspection contingencies. They protect the parties in case agreed-upon conditions are not met.

Disclosure Clauses

Federal law requires certain disclosures, such as the presence of lead paint, but states often have additional requirements.

Inspection Clauses

These should specify the type of inspection, who will conduct it, and what will happen if issues are found.

Arbitration Clauses

These require parties to resolve disputes through arbitration rather than through court litigation.

- Breach of Contract and Remedies

Types of Breach

Material Breach: A significant failure in performance.
Minor Breach: A less severe failure.

Remedies for Breach

Liquidated Damages: Pre-agreed upon damages set in the contract.

Rescission: The contract is canceled, and both parties are returned to their original positions.

- Conclusion

Contracts are a complex but essential part of real estate transactions. Understanding the various types, elements, and common clauses is crucial for anyone involved in the industry. This chapter should serve as a comprehensive guide, providing you with the knowledge you need to navigate contracts in your real estate endeavors.

Mock Exam Contracts

→1. What is the primary purpose of a Purchase Agreement in real estate?

A. To outline the commission for the real estate agent
B. To set the stage for the relationship between buyer and seller
C. To provide a warranty for the property
D. To list the property on MLS

Answer: B

The Purchase Agreement serves as the cornerstone of any real estate transaction, outlining the terms and conditions between the buyer and seller.

→2. Which type of lease requires the tenant to pay a flat rent while the landlord pays for all property charges?

A. Gross Lease
B. Net Lease
C. Triple Net Lease
D. Modified Gross Lease

Answer: A

In a Gross Lease, the tenant pays a flat rent and the landlord is responsible for all property charges.

→3. What is "Consideration" in a contract?

A. A thoughtful gesture
B. Money or something of value exchanged
C. A legal requirement
D. A counteroffer

Answer: B

Consideration refers to something of value that is exchanged between parties in a contract. It can be money, services, or even a promise.

➙4. What happens in a Material Breach of contract?

A. A minor failure in performance
B. A significant failure in performance
C. A legal dispute
D. Contract is automatically renewed

Answer: B

A Material Breach is a significant failure in performance that allows the other party to seek remedies.

➙5. Which clause in a contract specifies what will happen if issues are found during an inspection?

A. Contingency Clause
B. Disclosure Clause
C. Inspection Clause
D. Arbitration Clause

Answer: C

The Inspection Clause outlines the type of inspection, who will conduct it, and what actions will be taken if issues are found.

➙6. What does a "Straight Option" in an Option Agreement provide?

A. The right to lease the property
B. The exclusive right to purchase within a certain time
C. The right to sublease the property

D. The right to first refusal

Answer: B

A Straight Option gives the buyer the exclusive right to purchase the property within a specified time frame.

➡ 7. **Who cannot legally enter into a contract?**

A. A licensed real estate agent
B. A minor
C. A property manager
D. A real estate investor

Answer: B

Minors are not legally competent to enter into contracts.

➡ 8. **What is the primary purpose of Disclosure Clauses?**

A. To outline the commission structure
B. To state federal and state requirements for property disclosure
C. To specify the type of inspection
D. To set the rent amount in a lease

Answer: B

Disclosure Clauses are used to state federal and state requirements for property disclosure, such as the presence of lead paint.

➡ 9. **What is a Conditional Sale Agreement?**

A. The property is sold as-is
B. The sale is conditional upon certain criteria
C. The buyer has the option to purchase later

D. The seller can back out at any time

Answer: B

A Conditional Sale Agreement means the sale is conditional upon certain criteria being met, such as the sale of the buyer's current home.

➡10. What is the legal status of a contract for illegal activities?

A. Valid
B. Null and void
C. Conditional
D. Binding

Answer: B

Contracts for illegal activities are considered null and void.

➡11. What is the role of an "Escrow Agent" in a real estate contract?

A. To market the property
B. To hold and disburse funds
C. To conduct inspections
D. To negotiate terms

Answer: B

The Escrow Agent holds and disburses funds according to the terms of the contract.

➡12. Which of the following is NOT a required element for a contract to be valid?

A. Offer and acceptance
B. Consideration
C. Legal purpose
D. Notarization

Answer: D

Notarization is not a required element for a contract to be valid.

➡ **13. What is the "Statute of Frauds" in relation to contracts?**

A. A law that makes oral contracts illegal

B. A law that requires certain contracts to be in writing

C. A law that prevents fraudulent activities

D. A law that nullifies all previous contracts

Answer: B

The Statute of Frauds requires certain contracts, like those for real estate, to be in writing to be enforceable.

➡ **14. What does "Time is of the Essence" mean in a contract?**

A. The contract has no expiration date

B. The contract must be executed within a specific timeframe

C. The contract can be modified at any time

D. The contract is not urgent

Answer: B

"Time is of the Essence" means that the contract must be executed within a specific timeframe, and delays could lead to penalties or termination of the contract.

➡ **15. What is a "Right of First Refusal"?**

A. The right to reject any offer

B. The right to match or better any offer received by the seller

C. The right to be the first to view a property

D. The right to terminate a contract without penalty

Answer: B

The **Right of First Refusal** allows the holder to match or better any offer received by the seller before the property is sold to another party.

➡16. What is a "Contingent Contract"?

A. A contract that is dependent on certain conditions being met
B. A contract that is legally binding
C. A contract that has been terminated
D. A contract that is in the negotiation phase

Answer: A

A Contingent Contract is dependent on certain conditions being met, such as financing approval or a satisfactory home inspection.

➡17. What is "Specific Performance"?

A. A clause that specifies the responsibilities of each party
B. A legal remedy for breach of contract
C. A type of contract used in commercial real estate
D. A measure of a real estate agent's effectiveness

Answer: B

Specific Performance is a legal remedy that forces the breaching party to fulfill the terms of the contract.

➡18. What is the purpose of a "Hold Harmless Clause"?

A. To protect the buyer from market fluctuations
B. To protect one or both parties from liability for the actions of the other
C. To hold the property off the market for a specific period
D. To hold the buyer's deposit in escrow

Answer: B

A Hold Harmless Clause protects one or both parties from liability for the actions or negligence of the other party.

19. What is a "Bilateral Contract"?

A. A contract where only one party is obligated to perform
B. A contract where both parties are obligated to perform
C. A contract that is null and void
D. A contract that has been terminated

Answer: B

In a Bilateral Contract, both parties are obligated to perform their respective duties.

20. What is the "Implied Covenant of Good Faith and Fair Dealing"?

A. A written clause in every contract
B. An unwritten obligation for parties to act honestly and not cheat each other
C. A legal doctrine that makes all contracts public
D. A requirement for all contracts to be reviewed by a lawyer

Answer: B

The Implied Covenant of Good Faith and Fair Dealing is an unwritten obligation that requires parties to act honestly and not cheat or mislead each other.

21. What is a "Unilateral Contract"?

A. A contract where only one party is obligated to perform
B. A contract where both parties are obligated to perform
C. A contract that is null and void
D. A contract that has been terminated

Answer: A

In a Unilateral Contract, only one party is obligated to perform, while the other has the option but not the obligation to perform.

22. What is "Liquidated Damages"?

A. The actual damages suffered due to a breach

B. A pre-determined amount to be paid in case of a breach

C. The refundable part of a deposit

D. The non-refundable part of a deposit

Answer: B

Liquidated Damages are a pre-determined amount agreed upon by the parties to be paid in case of a breach of contract.

23. What is "Novation"?

A. The act of renewing a contract

B. The act of replacing one party in a contract with another

C. The act of nullifying a contract

D. The act of negotiating the terms of a contract

Answer: B

Novation is the act of replacing one party in a contract with another, effectively transferring the obligations to the new party.

24. What is an "Addendum"?

A. A change to the original contract

B. A separate agreement that is included with the original contract

C. A summary of the contract

D. A legal interpretation of the contract

Answer: B

An Addendum is a separate agreement that is included with the original contract to add or clarify terms.

➡ 25. What is "Recission"?

A. The act of renewing a contract
B. The act of terminating a contract and restoring parties to their original positions
C. The act of transferring a contract
D. The act of amending a contract

Answer: B

Recission is the act of terminating a contract and restoring the parties to their original positions, as if the contract had never existed.

➡ 26. What is "Parol Evidence"?

A. Written evidence
B. Oral evidence
C. Photographic evidence
D. Video evidence

Answer: B

Parol Evidence refers to oral statements or agreements that are not included in the written contract.

➡ 27. What is a "Counteroffer"?

A. An acceptance of the original offer
B. A rejection of the original offer
C. A new offer made in response to an original offer

D. A legal requirement for all contracts

Answer: C

A Counteroffer is a new offer made in response to an original offer, effectively rejecting the original offer.

28. What is "Earnest Money"?

A. Money paid to confirm a contract
B. Money paid to a real estate agent
C. Money held in escrow
D. Money paid for a home inspection

Answer: A

Earnest Money is money paid to confirm a contract, showing the buyer's serious intent to purchase.

29. What is "Force Majeure"?

A. A clause that frees both parties from liability in case of an extraordinary event
B. A clause that holds both parties liable regardless of circumstances
C. A clause that allows for price negotiation
D. A clause that requires a third-party mediator

Answer: A

Force Majeure is a clause that frees both parties from liability in case of an extraordinary event, like a natural disaster, that prevents one or both parties from fulfilling the contract.

30. What is "Severability"?

A. The ability to separate a contract into individual clauses
B. The ability to terminate a contract without penalty

C. The ability to transfer a contract to another party

D. The ability to amend a contract after signing

Answer: A

Severability is the ability to separate a contract into individual clauses, so that if one clause is found to be unenforceable, the rest of the contract remains in effect.

➡ 31. What does "Statute of Frauds" require for a real estate contract to be enforceable?

A. Verbal agreement

B. Written and signed agreement

C. Notarized agreement

D. Witnessed agreement

Answer: B

The Statute of Frauds requires that a real estate contract must be in writing and signed by the parties to be enforceable.

➡ 32. What is "Specific Performance"?

A. Monetary compensation for breach of contract

B. Forcing a party to carry out the terms of the contract

C. Nullifying the contract

D. Amending the contract

Answer: B

Specific Performance is a legal remedy that forces a party to carry out the terms of the contract as agreed.

➡ 33. What is "Time is of the Essence" in a contract?

A. A clause that allows for flexible deadlines

B. A clause that makes deadlines strictly binding

C. A clause that nullifies the contract after a certain time

D. A clause that allows for automatic renewal of the contract

answer: B

"Time is of the Essence" is a clause that makes deadlines strictly binding, and failure to meet them could lead to breach of contract.

34. What is an "Open Listing"?

A. A listing agreement with multiple brokers

B. A listing agreement with one broker

C. A listing that is not publicly advertised

D. A listing that is only advertised within a brokerage

Answer: A

An Open Listing is a listing agreement where the seller can employ multiple brokers who can bring buyers to the property.

35. What is a "Net Listing"?

A. A listing where the broker's commission is a percentage of the sale price

B. A listing where the broker keeps all amounts above a certain price

C. A listing where the broker charges a flat fee

D. A listing where the broker's commission is paid by the buyer

Answer: B

In a Net Listing, the broker agrees to sell the owner's property for a set price, and anything above that price is kept as the broker's commission.

36. What is a "Contingency" in a contract?

A. A fixed term

B. A condition that must be met for the contract to be binding

C. A penalty for breach of contract

D. An optional term

Answer: B

A Contingency is a condition that must be met for the contract to proceed to closing.

37. What is "Due Diligence" in the context of a real estate contract?

A. The buyer's investigation of the property

B. The seller's disclosure of property defects

C. The broker's marketing efforts

D. The lender's appraisal of the property

Answer: A

Due Diligence refers to the buyer's investigation of the property to discover any issues that were not disclosed.

38. What is "Escrow"?

A. A legal process to resolve disputes

B. A third-party account where funds are held until conditions are met

C. A type of mortgage

D. A tax levied on property sales

Answer: B

Escrow is a third-party account where funds or assets are held until contractual conditions are met.

39. What is "Right of First Refusal"?

A. The right to be the first to purchase a property

B. The right to refuse any offer on a property

C. The right to terminate a contract

D. The right to amend a contract

Answer: A

Right of First Refusal gives a person the opportunity to be the first to purchase a property before the owner sells it to someone else.

⇢ 40. What is "Joint Tenancy"?

A. Ownership by one individual

B. Ownership by two or more individuals with equal shares

C. Ownership by a corporation

D. Ownership by tenants

Answer: B

Joint Tenancy is a form of ownership where two or more individuals own property with equal shares and have the right of survivorship.

⇢ 41. What is the primary purpose of a "Letter of Intent" in a real estate transaction?

A. To serve as a binding contract

B. To outline the terms under which a contract will be negotiated

C. To legally transfer property

D. To terminate an existing contract

Answer: B

A Letter of Intent serves to outline the terms under which the parties will negotiate a contract. It is generally not binding.

42. What does "Time is of the Essence" mean in a real estate contract?

A. The contract has an indefinite period
B. The contract must be executed within a specific timeframe
C. The contract can be terminated at any time
D. The contract is not time-sensitive

Answer: B

"Time is of the Essence" means that the contract must be executed within a specific timeframe, and failure to do so could result in penalties or termination of the contract.

43. What is the purpose of an "Addendum" in a real estate contract?

A. To correct a typo or error
B. To add additional terms or conditions
C. To terminate the contract
D. To renew the contract

Answer: B

An Addendum is used to add additional terms or conditions to an existing contract, effectively modifying it.

44. What is the effect of a "Waiver" in a contract?

A. It adds a new term to the contract
B. It removes a party's right to enforce a term of the contract
C. It extends the contract's duration
D. It makes the contract voidable

Answer: B

A waiver removes a party's right to enforce a particular term of the contract, essentially giving up that right.

➡ 45. What is "Specific Performance" in the context of a real estate contract?

A. Monetary compensation
B. Carrying out the exact terms of the contract
C. Termination of the contract
D. An optional performance

Answer: B

Specific Performance refers to carrying out the exact terms of the contract, usually enforced through a court order.

➡ 46. What does "Novation" mean in a contract?

A. Renewal of the contract
B. Replacement of one party with another
C. Addition of a new term
D. Termination of the contract

Answer: B

Novation means the replacement of one party in the contract with another, effectively transferring the obligations to the new party.

➡ 47. What does "Force Majeure" refer to in a contract?

A. A type of fraud
B. An act of God or unforeseen circumstances
C. A breach of contract
D. A type of contingency

Answer: B

Force Majeure refers to unforeseen circumstances or "acts of God" that prevent one or both parties from fulfilling the contract. It usually allows for the contract to be terminated or suspended.

48. What is the role of an "Escrow Agent"?

A. To negotiate the contract
B. To hold and disburse funds or documents
C. To enforce the contract
D. To terminate the contract

Answer: B
An Escrow Agent holds and disburses funds or documents as per the terms of the contract.

49. What is "Right of First Refusal" in a real estate contract?

A. The right to back out of the contract first
B. The right to match any offer received by the seller
C. The right to inspect the property first
D. The right to make the first offer on a property

Answer: B
Right of First Refusal gives a party the right to match any offer received by the seller, usually before the property is sold to another buyer.

50. What is "Earnest Money" in the context of a real estate contract?

A. The commission for the real estate agent
B. A deposit made by the buyer to show good faith
C. The final payment made at closing
D. A refundable deposit

Answer: B

Earnest Money is a deposit made by the buyer to show good faith and secure the contract. It is usually non-refundable and is applied to the purchase price.

Real Estate Calculations

Real estate calculations are an integral part of the real estate industry. Whether you're an agent, a buyer, or an investor, understanding the numbers is crucial. This chapter will delve into the most important calculations you'll encounter, from mortgage payments to investment returns.

Property Valuation

- Comparative Market Analysis (CMA)

A Comparative Market Analysis (CMA) is the cornerstone of property valuation. It involves comparing the property in question to similar properties ("comparables" or "comps") that have recently sold in the area.

Formula:

Property Value = Average Price of Comparable Properties x (1 + Adjustment Factor)}

Why It Matters:
Understanding how to accurately perform a CMA can mean the difference between overpricing a property, causing it to sit on the market, or underpricing it and losing money.

- Capitalization Rate

The capitalization rate, or cap rate, is another essential metric for property valuation, particularly for income-generating properties.

Formula:

$$\text{Cap Rate} = \frac{Net\ Operating\ Income}{Current\ Market\ Value}$$

Why It Matters:

The cap rate gives you a quick way to compare the profitability of different investment properties.

Financing Calculations

- Mortgage Payments

Mortgage calculations are essential for both buyers and real estate professionals to understand.

Formula:

$$M = P \times \frac{r(1+r)^n}{(1+r)^n - 1}$$

Where :

M is the monthly payment,

P is the principal loan amount,

r is the monthly interest rate, and

n is the number of payments.

Why It Matters:

Knowing how to calculate mortgage payments allows you to assess the affordability of a property and helps in planning long-term finances.

- Loan-to-Value Ratio (LTV)

The Loan-to-Value ratio is a risk assessment metric that lenders use.

Formula:

$$\text{LTV} = \frac{\text{Loan Amount}}{\text{Appraised Value}} \times 100$$

Why It Matters:

A high LTV ratio might mean a riskier loan from a lender's perspective, potentially requiring the borrower to purchase mortgage insurance.

Investment Calculations

- Return on Investment (ROI)

ROI is a measure of the profitability of an investment.

Formula:

$$ROI = \frac{Net\ Profit}{Cost\ of\ Investment} \times 100$$

Why It Matters:

ROI gives you a snapshot of the investment's performance, helping you compare it against other investment opportunities.

- Cash-on-Cash Return

This metric gives you the annual return on your investment based on the cash flow and the amount of money you've invested.

Formula:

$$Cash\text{-}on\text{-}Cash\ Return = \frac{Annual\ Cash\ Flow}{Total\ Cash\ Invested} \times 100$$

Why It Matters:

Cash-on-cash return is crucial for understanding the cash income you're generating compared to the cash invested, providing a more accurate picture of an investment's performance.

Area and Volume Calculations

- Square Footage

Square footage is the measure of an area, and it's one of the most basic calculations in real estate.

Formula:

Area = Length x Width

Why It Matters:
Square footage affects everything from listing prices to renovation costs, so getting it right is crucial.

- Cubic Footage

Cubic footage is often used in commercial real estate to determine the volume of a space.

Formula:

Volume = Length x Width x Height

Why It Matters:
In commercial settings, cubic footage can be essential for understanding how a space can be used.

Prorations and Commissions

- Prorations

Prorations are used to divide property taxes, insurance premiums, or other costs between the buyer and seller.

Formula:

Proration Amount = $\frac{Annual\ Cost}{365}$ **x Number of Days**

Why It Matters:
Prorations ensure that both parties are only paying for their share of the costs during the time they own the property.

- Commission Calculation

Commissions are the lifeblood of most real estate agents and brokers.

Formula:

Commission = Sale Price x Commission Rate

Why It Matters:
Understanding how commissions are calculated can help agents set realistic business goals and expectations.

Conclusion

Mastering these calculations is not just a requirement for passing various real estate exams; it's a necessity for a successful career in real estate. This chapter has covered the essential calculations any real estate professional needs to understand.

Mock Exam Real Estate Calculations

→1. What is the formula for calculating the Loan-to-Value ratio?

   A. Loan Amount / Appraised Value

   B. Appraised Value / Loan Amount

   C. Loan Amount × Appraised Value

   D. Appraised Value × Loan Amount

Answer: A

The Loan-to-Value ratio is calculated as Loan Amount divided by Appraised Value.

→2. What does ROI stand for?

   A. Return On Investment

   B. Rate Of Interest

   C. Real Estate Opportunity

   D. Rate Of Inflation

Answer: A

ROI stands for Return On Investment, which measures the profitability of an investment.

→3. What is the formula for calculating square footage?

   A. Length × Width

   B. Length × Height

   C. Length + Width

   D. Length / Width

Answer: A

Square footage is calculated by multiplying the length by the width of the area.

▶ 4. What is the formula for calculating mortgage payments?

A. $P \times (r(1+r)^n) / ((1+r)^n - 1)$
B. $P \times r \times n$
C. $P / r \times n$
D. $P \times n / r$

Answer: A

The formula for calculating mortgage payments is $P \times (r(1+r)^n) / ((1+r)^n - 1)$.

▶ 5. What is the formula for calculating the capitalization rate?

A. Net Operating Income / Current Market Value
B. Current Market Value / Net Operating Income
C. Net Operating Income × Current Market Value
D. Current Market Value × Net Operating Income

Answer: A

The capitalization rate is calculated as Net Operating Income divided by Current Market Value.

▶ 6. What does CMA stand for in real estate calculations?

A. Comparative Market Analysis
B. Capital Market Assessment
C. Current Market Appraisal
D. Comparative Monetary Assessment

Answer: A

CMA stands for Comparative Market Analysis, used for property valuation.

➡7. What is the formula for calculating Cash-on-Cash Return?

    A. Annual Cash Flow / Total Cash Invested × 100
    B. Total Cash Invested / Annual Cash Flow × 100
    C. Annual Cash Flow × Total Cash Invested
    D. Total Cash Invested × Annual Cash Flow

Answer: A

Cash-on-Cash Return is calculated as Annual Cash Flow divided by Total Cash Invested, multiplied by 100.

➡8. What is the formula for calculating prorations?

    A. Annual Cost / 365 × Number of Days
    B. Annual Cost × 365 / Number of Days
    C. Number of Days / Annual Cost × 365
    D. Number of Days × Annual Cost / 365

Answer: A

Prorations are calculated as Annual Cost divided by 365, multiplied by the Number of Days.

➡9. What is the formula for calculating cubic footage?

    A. Length × Width × Height
    B. Length × Width
    C. Length × Height
    D. Width × Height

Answer: A

Cubic footage is calculated by multiplying the length, width, and height of the space.

➡10. What is the formula for calculating commissions?

A. Sale Price × Commission Rate

B. Commission Rate × Sale Price

C. Sale Price / Commission Rate

D. Commission Rate / Sale Price

Answer: A

Commissions are calculated as Sale Price multiplied by Commission Rate.

11. What is the formula for calculating Gross Rent Multiplier (GRM)?

A. Property Price / Gross Annual Rents

B. Gross Annual Rents / Property Price

C. Property Price × Gross Annual Rents

D. Gross Annual Rents × Property Price

Answer: A

The Gross Rent Multiplier (GRM) is calculated by dividing the property price by the gross annual rents.

12. What is the formula for calculating depreciation?

A. (Cost of the Property - Salvage Value) / Useful Life

B. (Salvage Value - Cost of the Property) / Useful Life

C. Cost of the Property × Salvage Value

D. Salvage Value × Cost of the Property

Answer: A

Depreciation is calculated by subtracting the salvage value from the cost of the property and dividing by its useful life.

13. What does PITI stand for in mortgage calculations?

A. Principal, Interest, Taxes, Insurance
B. Payment, Interest, Taxes, Insurance
C. Principal, Income, Taxes, Insurance
D. Payment, Income, Taxes, Insurance

Answer: A

PITI stands for Principal, Interest, Taxes, and Insurance, which are the four components of a mortgage payment.

➙14. What is the formula for calculating equity?

A. Market Value - Mortgage Balance
B. Mortgage Balance - Market Value
C. Market Value × Mortgage Balance
D. Mortgage Balance × Market Value

Answer: A

Equity is calculated as the market value of the property minus the mortgage balance.

➙15. What is the formula for calculating net operating income (NOI)?

A. Gross Income - Operating Expenses
B. Operating Expenses - Gross Income
C. Gross Income × Operating Expenses
D. Operating Expenses × Gross Income

Answer: A

Net Operating Income (NOI) is calculated by subtracting operating expenses from gross income.

➙16. What is the formula for calculating the break-even point?

A. Fixed Costs / (Selling Price - Variable Costs)

B. (Selling Price - Variable Costs) / Fixed Costs

C. Fixed Costs × (Selling Price - Variable Costs)

D. (Selling Price - Variable Costs) × Fixed Costs

Answer: A

The break-even point is calculated by dividing fixed costs by the difference between the selling price and variable costs.

➡ 17. What is the formula for calculating the internal rate of return (IRR)?

A. NPV = 0

B. ROI = 100%

C. NPV × ROI

D. ROI × NPV

Answer: A

The internal rate of return (IRR) is the discount rate that makes the net present value (NPV) of all cash flows equal to zero.

➡ 18. What is the formula for calculating the price per square foot?

A. Total Price / Total Square Footage

B. Total Square Footage / Total Price

C. Total Price × Total Square Footage

D. Total Square Footage × Total Price

Answer: A.

The price per square foot is calculated by dividing the total price by the total square footage.

➡ 19. What is the formula for calculating the amortization schedule?

A. $P \times (r(1+r)^n) / ((1+r)^n - 1)$

B. P × r × n

C. P / r × n

D. P × n / r

Answer: A

The formula for calculating the amortization schedule is P × (r(1+r)^n) / ((1+r)^n-1).

20. What is the formula for calculating the future value of an investment?

A. P × (1 + r)^n

B. P × (1 - r)^n

C. P / (1 + r)^n

D. P / (1 - r)^n

Answer: A

The future value of an investment is calculated as P × (1 + r)^n.

21. How do you calculate the Net Operating Income (NOI) for a property?

A. Gross Income - Operating Expenses

B. Gross Income + Operating Expenses

C. Operating Expenses - Gross Income

D. Gross Income × Operating Expenses

Answer: A

Net Operating Income is calculated by subtracting the operating expenses from the gross income.

22. What is the formula for calculating the loan-to-value ratio (LTV)?

A. Mortgage Amount / Appraised Value

B. Appraised Value / Mortgage Amount

C. Mortgage Amount × Appraised Value

D. Appraised Value × Mortgage Amount

Answer: A

The loan-to-value ratio (LTV) is calculated by dividing the mortgage amount by the appraised value of the property.

23. What is the formula for calculating the cash-on-cash return?

A. Annual Pre-tax Cash Flow / Total Cash Invested

B. Total Cash Invested / Annual Pre-tax Cash Flow

C. Annual Pre-tax Cash Flow × Total Cash Invested

D. Total Cash Invested × Annual Pre-tax Cash Flow

Answer: A

The cash-on-cash return is calculated by dividing the annual pre-tax cash flow by the total cash invested.

24. What is the formula for calculating the debt service coverage ratio (DSCR)?

A. Net Operating Income / Debt Service

B. Debt Service / Net Operating Income

C. Net Operating Income × Debt Service

D. Debt Service × Net Operating Income

Answer: A

The debt service coverage ratio (DSCR) is calculated by dividing the net operating income by the debt service.

25. What is the formula for calculating the equity build-up rate?

A. (Principal Paid in Year 1 / Initial Investment) × 100

B. (Initial Investment / Principal Paid in Year 1) × 100

C. Principal Paid in Year 1 × Initial Investment

D. Initial Investment × Principal Paid in Year 1

Answer: A

The equity build-up rate is calculated by dividing the principal paid in the first year by the initial investment and then multiplying by 100.

26. What is the formula for calculating the gross operating income (GOI)?

A. Gross Potential Income - Vacancy and Credit Losses

B. Vacancy and Credit Losses - Gross Potential Income

C. Gross Potential Income × Vacancy and Credit Losses

D. Vacancy and Credit Losses × Gross Potential Income

Answer: A

The gross operating income (GOI) is calculated by subtracting vacancy and credit losses from the gross potential income.

27. What is the formula for calculating the effective gross income (EGI)?

A. Gross Operating Income + Other Income

B. Other Income - Gross Operating Income

C. Gross Operating Income × Other Income

D. Other Income × Gross Operating Income

Answer: A

The effective gross income (EGI) is calculated by adding other income to the gross operating income.

28. What is the formula for calculating the absorption rate?

A. Number of Units Sold / Number of Units Available

B. Number of Units Available / Number of Units Sold

C. Number of Units Sold × Number of Units Available

D. Number of Units Available × Number of Units Sold

Answer: A

The absorption rate is calculated by dividing the number of units sold by the number of units available.

➡ 29. What is the formula for calculating the price-to-rent ratio?

A. Home Price / Annual Rent

B. Annual Rent / Home Price

C. Home Price × Annual Rent

D. Annual Rent × Home Price

Answer: A

The price-to-rent ratio is calculated by dividing the home price by the annual rent.

➡ 30. What is the formula for calculating the yield?

A. Annual Income / Investment Cost

B. Investment Cost / Annual Income

C. Annual Income × Investment Cost

D. Investment Cost × Annual Income

Answer: A

The yield is calculated by dividing the annual income by the investment cost.

➡ 31. What is the formula for calculating the Gross Rent Multiplier (GRM)?

A. Sales Price / Monthly Rent

B. Monthly Rent / Sales Price

C. Sales Price × Monthly Rent

D. Monthly Rent × Sales Price

Answer: A

The Gross Rent Multiplier (GRM) is calculated by dividing the sales price by the monthly rent.

32. How do you calculate the Loan-to-Value ratio (LTV)?

A. Loan Amount / Appraised Value

B. Appraised Value / Loan Amount

C. Loan Amount × Appraised Value

D. Appraised Value × Loan Amount

Answer: A

The Loan-to-Value ratio (LTV) is calculated by dividing the loan amount by the appraised value of the property.

33. How do you calculate the Net Operating Income (NOI)?

A. Gross Operating Income - Operating Expenses

B. Operating Expenses - Gross Operating Income

C. Gross Operating Income × Operating Expenses

D. Operating Expenses × Gross Operating Income

Answer: A

The Net Operating Income (NOI) is calculated by subtracting the operating expenses from the gross operating income.

34. How do you calculate the Debt Service Coverage Ratio (DSCR)?

A. Net Operating Income / Debt Service

B. Debt Service / Net Operating Income

C. Net Operating Income × Debt Service

D. Debt Service × Net Operating Income

Answer: A

The Debt Service Coverage Ratio (DSCR) is calculated by dividing the Net Operating Income by the Debt Service.

35. What is the formula for calculating the Break-Even Ratio (BER)?

A. (Operating Expenses + Debt Service) / Gross Operating Income

B. Gross Operating Income / (Operating Expenses + Debt Service)

C. (Operating Expenses + Debt Service) × Gross Operating Income

D. Gross Operating Income × (Operating Expenses + Debt Service)

Answer: A

The Break-Even Ratio (BER) is calculated by dividing the sum of operating expenses and debt service by the gross operating income.

36. How do you calculate the Effective Gross Income (EGI)?

A. Gross Income - Vacancy Losses + Other Income

B. Gross Income + Vacancy Losses - Other Income

C. Gross Income × Vacancy Losses + Other Income

D. Gross Income + Vacancy Losses × Other Income

Answer: A

The Effective Gross Income (EGI) is calculated by subtracting vacancy losses from the gross income and adding any other income.

37. What is the formula for calculating the Operating Expense Ratio (OER)?

A. Operating Expenses / Effective Gross Income

B. Effective Gross Income / Operating Expenses

C. Operating Expenses × Effective Gross Income

D. Effective Gross Income × Operating Expenses

Answer: A

The **Operating Expense Ratio (OER)** is calculated by dividing the operating expenses by the effective gross income.

➡ 38. How do you calculate the Cash-on-Cash Return?

A. Cash Flow Before Taxes / Initial Investment

B. Initial Investment / Cash Flow Before Taxes

C. Cash Flow Before Taxes × Initial Investment

D. Initial Investment × Cash Flow Before Taxes

Answer: A

The **Cash-on-Cash Return** is calculated by dividing the cash flow before taxes by the initial investment.

➡ 39. What is the formula for calculating the Amortization Factor?

A. Monthly Payment / Loan Amount

B. Loan Amount / Monthly Payment

C. Monthly Payment × Loan Amount

D. Loan Amount × Monthly Payment

Answer: A

The **Amortization Factor** is calculated by dividing the monthly payment by the loan amount.

➡ 40. How do you calculate the Equity Dividend Rate (EDR)?

A. Cash Flow After Taxes / Equity Investment

B. Equity Investment / Cash Flow After Taxes

C. Cash Flow After Taxes × Equity Investment

D. Equity Investment × Cash Flow After Taxes

41. What is the formula for calculating the Debt Service Coverage Ratio (DSCR)?

A. Net Operating Income / Debt Service

B. Debt Service / Net Operating Income

C. Net Operating Income × Debt Service

D. Debt Service - Net Operating Income

Answer: A

The Debt Service Coverage Ratio is calculated by dividing the Net Operating Income by the Debt Service.

42. How do you calculate the Gross Rent Multiplier (GRM)?

A. Property Price / Monthly Rent

B. Monthly Rent / Property Price

C. Annual Rent / Property Price

D. Property Price / Annual Rent

Answer: A

The Gross Rent Multiplier is calculated by dividing the property price by the monthly rent.

43. What is the formula for calculating Loan-to-Value ratio?

A. Loan Amount / Property Value

B. Property Value / Loan Amount

C. Loan Amount × Property Value

D. Property Value - Loan Amount

Answer: A

The Loan-to-Value ratio is calculated by dividing the loan amount by the property value.

➡ 44. How do you calculate the break-even point in a real estate investment?

A. Fixed Costs / (Selling Price - Variable Costs)
B. (Selling Price - Variable Costs) / Fixed Costs
C. Fixed Costs × Selling Price
D. Selling Price / Fixed Costs

Answer: A

The break-even point is calculated by dividing the fixed costs by the difference between the selling price and variable costs.

➡ 45. How do you calculate the Return on Investment (ROI) for a property?

A. (Net Profit / Investment Cost) × 100
B. (Investment Cost / Net Profit) × 100
C. Net Profit × Investment Cost
D. Investment Cost - Net Profit

Answer: A

The Return on Investment is calculated by dividing the net profit by the investment cost and then multiplying by 100.

➡ 46. How do you calculate the equity in a property?

A. Property Value - Mortgage Balance
B. Mortgage Balance - Property Value
C. Property Value × Mortgage Balance
D. Mortgage Balance / Property Value

Answer: A

Equity is calculated by subtracting the mortgage balance from the property value.

➡ 47. What is the formula for calculating the amortization payment?

A. Principal Amount / Number of Payments

B. Interest Rate / Number of Payments

C. (Principal Amount × Interest Rate) / Number of Payments

D. (Principal Amount × Interest Rate) / (1 - (1 + Interest Rate)^-Number of Payments)

Answer: D

The amortization payment is calculated using the formula mentioned.

➡ 48. What is the formula for calculating the Internal Rate of Return (IRR) for a real estate investment?

A. The discount rate that makes the Net Present Value zero

B. The rate that equals the Net Operating Income

C. The rate that equals the Debt Service

D. The rate that makes the Gross Income zero

Answer: A

The Internal Rate of Return is the discount rate that makes the Net Present Value of all cash flows from a particular investment equal to zero.

➡ 49. What is the formula for calculating the rate of return on an investment property?

A. (Net Profit / Cost of Investment) × 100

B. (Cost of Investment / Net Profit) × 100

C. Net Profit × Cost of Investment

D. Cost of Investment - Net Profit

Answer: A

The rate of return is calculated by dividing the net profit by the cost of the investment and then multiplying by 100.

➡ 50. How do you calculate the net profit from a real estate investment?

A. Selling Price - (Buying Price + Costs)
B. (Buying Price + Costs) - Selling Price
C. Selling Price × Buying Price
D. Buying Price / Selling Price

Answer: A

The Net Operating Income (NOI) is calculated by subtracting the operating expenses from the gross operating income.

Specialty Areas

Real estate is a dynamic and multifaceted industry that offers a myriad of opportunities for professionals. The sector is divided into various specialty areas, each with its unique characteristics, requirements, and challenges. This chapter aims to delve deep into these specialty areas, providing you with a comprehensive understanding that can guide your career choices.

- Residential Real Estate

Overview

Residential real estate is perhaps the most familiar to the general public. It involves the buying, selling, and renting of properties designed for individual or family living. This sector is often the entry point for many new agents and brokers.

Types of Properties

Single-Family Homes: These are stand-alone houses designed for one family.
Condominiums: Individual units in a larger complex, often with shared amenities.
Townhouses: Multi-floor homes that share one or two walls with adjacent properties.
Multi-Family Homes: Buildings designed to house multiple families, such as duplexes and apartment buildings.

Skills Required

Strong Interpersonal Skills: Building relationships with clients is crucial.
Local Market Knowledge: Understanding the local market trends, school districts, and community features.
Negotiation Skills: Ability to negotiate favorable terms for clients.

Regulatory Aspects

- Fair Housing Laws
- Local zoning regulations
- Property taxes

- Commercial Real Estate

Overview

Commercial real estate focuses on properties used for business activities. These can range from small office spaces to large retail complexes. The stakes are often higher, and the deals more complex.

Types of Properties

Office Buildings: These can be small office complexes or large skyscrapers.
Retail Centers: These include shopping malls, strip malls, and standalone shops.
Warehouses: Used for storage and distribution.

Skills Required

Financial Analysis: Understanding balance sheets, income statements, and cash flow.
Understanding of Zoning Laws: Knowing what activities can be legally conducted in certain spaces.
Long-term Client Relationships: Commercial real estate often involves long-term leases, requiring a long-term relationship with clients.

Regulatory Aspects

- Commercial zoning laws
- Environmental regulations

- Lease agreements

- Industrial Real Estate

Overview

Industrial real estate is geared towards manufacturing, production, and distribution. These properties are often located in designated industrial zones and come with their own set of challenges and opportunities.

Types of Properties

Factories: Where goods are manufactured.
Distribution Centers: Where goods are stored and distributed.
Warehouses: Used for storage.

Skills Required

Knowledge of Industrial Machinery: Understanding the specific needs of industrial operations.
Understanding of Supply Chain Logistics: Knowing how the property fits into the client's larger operational framework.
Regulatory Compliance: Adhering to safety and environmental regulations.

Regulatory Aspects

- Industrial zoning laws
- Occupational Safety and Health Administration (OSHA) regulations
- Environmental Protection Agency (EPA) regulations

- Luxury Real Estate

Overview

Luxury real estate focuses on high-end, exclusive properties that are often priced well above the average market value. Agents in this sector often deal with high-net-worth individuals and must offer a level of service that matches the price tag of the properties they handle.

Types of Properties

Mansions: Large, opulent homes often with extensive grounds.
Penthouses: High-end apartments located on the top floors of high-rise buildings.
Historic Homes: Properties with historical significance and unique architectural features.

Skills Required

Discretion and Confidentiality: Clients in this sector value their privacy highly.
High-level Negotiation Skills: The stakes are high, and the margins can be significant.
Extensive Network: Knowing the right people can make or break a deal.

Regulatory Aspects

- Luxury tax implications
- Historic preservation regulations
- Privacy laws

- Conclusion

Choosing a specialty in real estate is a significant decision that can shape your career. Each area comes with its own set of challenges, opportunities, and rewards. Whether you're drawn to the fast-paced world of commercial real estate, the intricate challenges of industrial properties, or the high-stakes game of luxury homes, understanding the nuances of each specialty area can equip you with the knowledge you need to succeed. This chapter serves as a comprehensive guide, offering you the insights you need to make an informed choice about your career path in real estate.

Mock Exam Specialty Areas

➡1. Which type of real estate is often the entry point for many new agents and brokers?

   A. Commercial
   B. Industrial
   C. Residential
   D. Luxury

Answer: C. Residential

Explanation: The chapter states that residential real estate is often the entry point for many new agents and brokers.

➡2. What type of property is a penthouse?

   A. Industrial
   B. Commercial
   C. Residential
   D. Luxury

Answer: D. Luxury

Explanation: Penthouses are high-end apartments located on the top floors of high-rise buildings and fall under luxury real estate.

➡3. What is a key skill required in commercial real estate?

   A. Financial Analysis
   B. Knowledge of Industrial Machinery
   C. Strong Interpersonal Skills
   D. Discretion and Confidentiality

Answer: A. Financial Analysis

Explanation: Financial analysis is crucial in commercial real estate for understanding balance sheets, income statements, and cash flow.

4. What type of property is a factory?

A. Commercial
B. Industrial
C. Residential
D. Luxury

Answer: B. Industrial

Explanation: Factories are geared towards manufacturing, production, and distribution, which falls under industrial real estate.

5. What is a key regulatory aspect in industrial real estate?

A. Luxury tax implications
B. OSHA regulations
C. Fair Housing Laws
D. Commercial zoning laws

Answer: B. OSHA regulations

Explanation: Occupational Safety and Health Administration (OSHA) regulations are key in industrial real estate.

6. What type of property is a shopping mall?

A. Commercial
B. Industrial

C. Residential

D. Luxury

Answer: A. Commercial

Explanation: Shopping malls fall under commercial real estate as they are used for business activities.

➡ 7. What is a key skill required in luxury real estate?

A. Financial Analysis

B. Knowledge of Industrial Machinery

C. Strong Interpersonal Skills

D. Discretion and Confidentiality

Answer: D. Discretion and Confidentiality

Explanation: Clients in the luxury sector value their privacy highly, making discretion and confidentiality key skills.

➡ 8. What type of property is a townhouse?

A. Commercial

B. Industrial

C. Residential

D. Luxury

Answer: C. Residential

Explanation: Townhouses are multi-floor homes designed for individual or family living, which falls under residential real estate.

➡ 9. What is a key regulatory aspect in residential real estate?

A. Luxury tax implications

B. OSHA regulations

C. Fair Housing Laws

D. Commercial zoning laws

Answer: C. Fair Housing Laws

Explanation: Fair Housing Laws are key regulatory aspects in residential real estate to ensure equal opportunity in housing.

10. What type of property is a distribution center?

A. Commercial

B. Industrial

C. Residential

D. Luxury

Answer: B. Industrial

Explanation: Distribution centers are used for storing and distributing goods, which falls under industrial real estate.

11. What type of real estate involves the sale of businesses?

A. Commercial

B. Business Brokerage

C. Residential

D. Luxury

Answer: B. Business Brokerage

Explanation: Business Brokerage involves the sale of businesses, including their assets and real estate.

12. What is a key skill required in business brokerage?

A. Negotiation Skills

B. Knowledge of Industrial Machinery

C. Strong Interpersonal Skills

D. Financial Analysis

Answer: A. Negotiation Skills

Explanation: Negotiation skills are crucial in business brokerage to secure the best deals for clients.

13. What type of real estate involves the sale of farmland?

A. Commercial

B. Industrial

C. Agricultural

D. Luxury

Answer: C. Agricultural

Explanation: Agricultural real estate involves the sale of farmland and agricultural facilities.

14. What is a key regulatory aspect in agricultural real estate?

A. EPA Regulations

B. OSHA regulations

C. Fair Housing Laws

D. Luxury tax implications

Answer: A. EPA Regulations

Explanation: Environmental Protection Agency (EPA) regulations are key in agricultural real estate.

➡ 15. What type of property is a hotel?

A. Commercial

B. Industrial

C. Residential

D. Hospitality

Answer: D. Hospitality

Explanation: Hotels fall under hospitality real estate, which is a sub-category of commercial real estate.

➡ 16. What is a key skill required in hospitality real estate?

A. Customer Service

B. Knowledge of Industrial Machinery

C. Strong Interpersonal Skills

D. Financial Analysis

Answer: A. Customer Service

Explanation: Customer service is crucial in hospitality real estate to ensure guest satisfaction.

➡ 17. What type of real estate involves the sale of undeveloped land?

A. Commercial

B. Land

C. Residential

D. Luxury

Answer: B. Land

Explanation: The sale of undeveloped land falls under land real estate.

➡ 18. What is a key regulatory aspect in land real estate?

A. Zoning Laws

B. OSHA regulations

C. Fair Housing Laws

D. Luxury tax implications

Answer: A. Zoning Laws

Explanation: Zoning laws are key in land real estate to determine the types of development that can occur.

19. What type of property is a condominium?

A. Commercial

B. Industrial

C. Residential

D. Luxury

Answer: C. Residential

Explanation: Condominiums are multi-unit properties that are sold individually, which falls under residential real estate.

20. What is a key skill required in land real estate?

A. Negotiation Skills

B. Knowledge of Zoning Laws

C. Strong Interpersonal Skills

D. Financial Analysis

Answer: B. Knowledge of Zoning Laws

Explanation: Knowledge of zoning laws is crucial in land real estate to guide clients on permissible uses.

21. What is the primary focus of industrial real estate?

A. Warehouses
B. Hotels
C. Farmland
D. Condominiums

Answer: A. Warehouses

Explanation: Industrial real estate primarily focuses on warehouses and manufacturing buildings.

22. What is a 1031 exchange commonly used for?

A. Residential properties
B. Commercial properties
C. Agricultural properties
D. Industrial properties

Answer: B. Commercial properties

Explanation: A 1031 exchange is commonly used to defer capital gains tax in commercial real estate.

23. What is the main consideration in retail real estate?

A. Location
B. Size
C. Zoning
D. Tax implications

Answer: A. Location

Explanation: Location is the main consideration in retail real estate, as it directly impacts customer footfall.

24. What is the primary focus of residential real estate?

A. Single-family homes

B. Warehouses

C. Hotels

D. Farmland

Answer: A. Single-family homes

Explanation: Residential real estate primarily focuses on single-family homes, although it can include multi-family units.

25. What is the main consideration in luxury real estate?

A. Price

B. Location

C. Amenities

D. Size

Answer: C. Amenities

Explanation: Luxury real estate often focuses on the amenities offered, such as pools, gyms, and concierge services.

26. What is the primary advantage of investing in mixed-use real estate?

A. Diversification

B. Lower taxes

C. Easier management

D. Higher rent

Answer: A. Diversification

Explanation: Mixed-use real estate offers diversification as it combines residential, commercial, and sometimes industrial spaces.

➡ 27. What is the main disadvantage of investing in vacation real estate?

A. Seasonal income
B. High maintenance
C. Zoning restrictions
D. High taxes

Answer: A. Seasonal income

Explanation: Vacation real estate often has seasonal income, which can be a disadvantage for consistent cash flow.

➡ 28. What is the primary consideration when investing in student housing?

A. Proximity to educational institutions
B. Luxury amenities
C. Tax benefits
D. Size of the property

Answer: A. Proximity to educational institutions

Explanation: The primary consideration for student housing is its proximity to educational institutions.

➡ 29. What is the main benefit of investing in senior living communities?

A. Lower maintenance
B. Steady income
C. Tax benefits
D. High rent

Answer: B. Steady income

Explanation: Senior living communities often provide a steady income due to long-term leases.

➡ 30. What is a triple net lease commonly used in?

A. Residential properties
B. Commercial properties
C. Industrial properties
D. Agricultural properties

Answer: B. Commercial properties

Explanation: A triple net lease is commonly used in commercial real estate, where the tenant pays property taxes, insurance, and maintenance costs.

➡ 31. What is the primary focus of hospitality real estate?

A. Hotels and resorts
B. Warehouses
C. Office buildings
D. Farmland

Answer: A. Hotels and resorts

Explanation: Hospitality real estate primarily focuses on hotels, resorts, and other lodging options.

➡ 32. What is the main consideration in agricultural real estate?

A. Soil quality
B. Location
C. Size
D. Zoning

Answer: A. Soil quality

Explanation: Soil quality is the main consideration in agricultural real estate for farming purposes.

33. What is the primary advantage of investing in REITs?

A. Liquidity

B. Control over property

C. Tax benefits

D. High rent

Answer: A. Liquidity

Explanation: REITs offer liquidity as they can be easily bought and sold on stock exchanges.

34. What is the main disadvantage of investing in office real estate?

A. High vacancy rates

B. Seasonal income

C. Zoning restrictions

D. High maintenance

Answer: A. High vacancy rates

Explanation: Office real estate can have high vacancy rates, especially in economic downturns.

35. What is the primary focus of mobile home parks?

A. Affordable housing

B. Luxury living

C. Commercial spaces

D. Agricultural land

Answer: A. Affordable housing

Explanation: Mobile home parks primarily focus on providing affordable housing options.

➡36. What is the primary consideration when investing in retail real estate?

A. Foot traffic

B. Tax benefits

C. Size of the property

D. Proximity to educational institutions

Answer: A. Foot traffic

Explanation: Foot traffic is crucial for the success of retail real estate.

➡37. What is the main benefit of investing in industrial real estate?

A. High rent

B. Long-term leases

C. Seasonal income

D. Tax benefits

Answer: B. Long-term leases

Explanation: Industrial real estate often comes with long-term leases, providing stable income.

➡38. What is a common disadvantage of investing in multi-family properties?

A. High maintenance costs

B. Low rent

C. Zoning restrictions

D. Seasonal income

Answer: A. High maintenance costs

Explanation: Multi-family properties often have higher maintenance costs due to multiple units.

39. What is the primary focus of medical real estate?

A. Hospitals and clinics
B. Office buildings
C. Warehouses
D. Hotels and resorts

Answer: A. Hospitals and clinics

Explanation: Medical real estate primarily focuses on hospitals, clinics, and other healthcare facilities.

40. What is the main consideration in raw land investment?

A. Zoning restrictions
B. Soil quality
C. Location
D. Size

Answer: C. Location

Explanation: Location is key in raw land investment for future development.

41. What is the primary advantage of investing in storage units?

A. Low maintenance
B. High rent
C. Tax benefits
D. Seasonal income

Answer: A. Low maintenance

Explanation: Storage units generally require low maintenance.

➡ 42. What is the main disadvantage of investing in co-working spaces?

   A. High vacancy rates
   B. Low rent
   C. Zoning restrictions
   D. Seasonal income

Answer: A. High vacancy rates

Explanation: Co-working spaces can have high vacancy rates, especially during economic downturns.

➡ 43. What is the primary focus of green real estate?

   A. Energy efficiency
   B. High rent
   C. Tax benefits
   D. Size of the property

Answer: A. Energy efficiency

Explanation: Green real estate primarily focuses on energy-efficient buildings.

➡ 44. What is the main benefit of investing in brownfield sites?

   A. Tax incentives
   B. High rent
   C. Seasonal income
   D. Long-term leases

Answer: A. Tax incentives

Explanation: Brownfield sites often come with tax incentives for redevelopment.

➡ **45. What is the primary consideration when investing in infill real estate?**

A. Location
B. Size
C. Zoning restrictions
D. Soil quality

Answer: A. Location

Explanation: Infill real estate focuses on developing vacant or underused parcels within existing urban areas, so location is key.

➡ **46. What is the main disadvantage of investing in luxury real estate?**

A. High maintenance costs
B. Seasonal income
C. Zoning restrictions
D. Low rent

Answer: A. High maintenance costs

Explanation: Luxury real estate often comes with high maintenance costs.

➡ **47. What is the primary focus of transit-oriented development?**

A. Proximity to public transport
B. Luxury amenities
C. Tax benefits
D. Size of the property

Answer: A. Proximity to public transport

Explanation: Transit-oriented development focuses on properties close to public transport facilities.

48. What is the main benefit of investing in adaptive reuse properties?

A. Tax incentives

B. High rent

C. Seasonal income

D. Long-term leases

Answer: A. Tax incentives

Explanation: Adaptive reuse properties often come with tax incentives for redevelopment.

49. What is the primary consideration when investing in distressed properties?

A. Cost of renovation

B. Location

C. Size

D. Zoning

Answer: A. Cost of renovation

Explanation: The cost of renovation is a key consideration when investing in distressed properties.

50. What is the main disadvantage of investing in fixer-uppers?

A. High renovation costs

B. Low rent

C. Zoning restrictions

D. Seasonal income

Answer: A. High renovation costs

Explanation: Fixer-uppers often come with high renovation costs that can eat into profits.

Ethics and Legal Considerations

Ethics and legal considerations are not just buzzwords in the real estate industry; they are the pillars that uphold the integrity and credibility of the profession. This chapter aims to dissect these complex yet indispensable aspects of real estate. We'll delve into the ethical frameworks that guide real estate professionals, explore the legal landscape that governs real estate transactions, and examine case studies that bring these concepts to life.

- Ethical Considerations

The Importance of Ethics in Real Estate

Ethics are the moral principles that govern behavior. In real estate, ethical considerations go beyond mere legality; they define how agents should conduct themselves in their professional relationships. Ethical behavior fosters trust, which is the cornerstone of any business, especially one that involves significant financial transactions like real estate.

Code of Ethics: A Closer Look

The National Association of Realtors (NAR) Code of Ethics is a comprehensive document that outlines the professional responsibilities of realtors. It is divided into three main categories: Duties to Clients and Customers, Duties to the Public, and Duties to Realtors. Each category has several articles that provide specific guidelines on various aspects like advertising, commissions, and dispute resolution.

Fiduciary Duties: Beyond the Basics

The fiduciary duties of loyalty, confidentiality, obedience, reasonable care, accounting, and full disclosure are not just legal requirements but ethical obligations. Each of these duties has a broader implication. For instance, 'reasonable care' means staying updated on market trends, legal changes, and other factors that could affect a client's decision.

Ethical Dilemmas and Resolutions

Real estate professionals often face ethical dilemmas, such as representing both the buyer and the seller in a transaction. The key to resolving such dilemmas lies in full disclosure, informed consent, and maintaining an unbiased stance.

- Legal Considerations

The Legal Landscape of Real Estate

The legal framework of real estate is a complex web of federal, state, and local laws. These laws cover various aspects, from property rights to contract law, and from fair housing to environmental regulations.

Licensing Laws: More Than Just a Certificate

Licensing laws are state-specific and dictate the requirements for becoming a real estate agent or broker. These laws often include educational qualifications, age criteria, background checks, and even specifications about the moral character of the applicant.

Contract Law: The Devil is in the Details

Contracts are the lifeblood of real estate transactions. Understanding the nuances of contract law, such as the elements that make a contract legally binding, can save professionals from legal complications down the line.

Zoning Laws and Environmental Regulations

Zoning laws can significantly impact a property's value and its intended use. Similarly, environmental regulations like wetland protections or historical site designations can affect a property transaction. Real estate professionals must be well-versed in these areas to guide their clients effectively.

Legal Case Studies

Case Study 1: The Legal Implications of Dual Agency

In this case, a dual agent faced a lawsuit for not adequately representing the interests of both the buyer and the seller. The court's ruling set a precedent for how dual agents should navigate the complexities of representing both parties.

Case Study 2: The Cost of Non-Disclosure

A seller and their agent faced legal repercussions for failing to disclose that a property was located in a flood zone. The case highlights the importance of full disclosure and the severe consequences of failing to adhere to it.

Conclusion

Ethics and legal considerations are not just checkboxes to tick off; they are ongoing commitments that require real estate professionals to continually educate themselves and make morally and legally sound decisions. This chapter has aimed to provide an in-depth understanding of these critical aspects, equipping you with the knowledge you need to uphold the highest standards of professionalism in your real estate career.

Mock Exam Ethics and Legal Considerations

➡1. What are the three main categories of the NAR Code of Ethics?

　A. Duties to Clients, Duties to Realtors, Duties to the Public

　B. Duties to Clients and Customers, Duties to the Public, Duties to Realtors

　C. Duties to Sellers, Duties to Buyers, Duties to the Public

　D. Duties to the Government, Duties to Clients, Duties to Realtors

Answer: B

The NAR Code of Ethics is divided into three main categories: Duties to Clients and Customers, Duties to the Public, and Duties to Realtors.

➡2. Which of the following is NOT a fiduciary duty?

　A. Loyalty

　B. Confidentiality

　C. Manipulation

　D. Full Disclosure

Answer: C

Manipulation is not a fiduciary duty. The fiduciary duties are loyalty, confidentiality, obedience, reasonable care, accounting, and full disclosure.

➡3. What is the primary purpose of zoning laws?

　A. To increase property taxes

　B. To regulate land use

　C. To protect endangered species

　D. To promote business

Answer: B

The primary purpose of zoning laws is to regulate land use, such as residential, commercial, or industrial zones.

➞ 4. What does 'reasonable care' in fiduciary duties imply?

   A. Taking vacations regularly
   B. Staying updated on market trends
   C. Investing in real estate
   D. Focusing on commission

Answer: B

'Reasonable care' means staying updated on market trends, legal changes, and other factors that could affect a client's decision.

➞ 5. What is the consequence of not adhering to full disclosure?

   A. Increased commission
   B. Legal repercussions
   C. More clients
   D. Promotion

Answer: B

Failing to adhere to full disclosure can lead to legal repercussions, including lawsuits and loss of license.

➞ 6. Which federal law is designed to ensure fair housing?

   A. The Sherman Act
   B. The Fair Housing Act
   C. The Clayton Act
   D. The Dodd-Frank Act

Answer: B

The Fair Housing Act is designed to prevent discrimination in housing based on race, color, religion, sex, or national origin.

➡ 7. What is the minimum age requirement for obtaining a real estate license in most states?

A. 16
B. 18
C. 21
D. 25

Answer: B

The minimum age requirement for obtaining a real estate license in most states is 18 years.

➡ 8. What is the key to resolving ethical dilemmas like dual agency?

A. Ignoring the issue
B. Full disclosure and informed consent
C. Choosing one party to represent
D. Consulting a lawyer

Answer: B

The key to resolving ethical dilemmas like dual agency lies in full disclosure and obtaining informed consent from all parties involved.

➡ 9. Which of the following is NOT an element that makes a contract legally binding?

A. Offer and acceptance

B. Consideration

C. Coercion

D. Legality of purpose

Answer: C

Coercion is not an element that makes a contract legally binding. A contract must have offer and acceptance, consideration, and legality of purpose to be legally binding.

➡ 10. What does the NAR Code of Ethics say about advertising?

A. It encourages aggressive advertising

B. It prohibits all forms of advertising

C. It requires truthful advertising

D. It promotes online advertising only

Answer: C

The NAR Code of Ethics requires that all advertising be truthful and not misleading.

➡ 11. What is the primary role of the Real Estate Commission in most states?

A. To sell properties

B. To regulate and license real estate agents

C. To build homes

D. To provide loans

Answer: B

The primary role of the Real Estate Commission in most states is to regulate and license real estate agents.

➡ 12. What is the statute of frauds?

A. A law that requires certain contracts to be in writing

B. A law that allows fraud in certain cases

C. A law that regulates online advertising

D. A law that deals with zoning issues

Answer: A

The statute of frauds is a law that requires certain contracts, like those for the sale of real estate, to be in writing to be enforceable.

13. What does RESPA stand for?

A. Real Estate Settlement Procedures Act

B. Real Estate Sales Professional Act

C. Residential Sales Property Act

D. Real Estate Security Policy Act

Answer: A

RESPA stands for Real Estate Settlement Procedures Act, which aims to provide transparency in the home buying process.

14. What is puffing in real estate terms?

A. Illegal misrepresentation

B. Exaggeration of property features

C. Accurate description of property

D. Undervaluing a property

Answer: B

Puffing refers to the exaggeration of property features, which is generally considered legal but can be ethically questionable.

15. What is the primary purpose of an escrow account?

A. To hold funds for investment

B. To hold funds until the completion of a real estate transaction

C. To pay for the agent's commission

D. To pay property taxes

Answer: B

The primary purpose of an escrow account is to hold funds until the completion of a real estate transaction.

16. What does the term "redlining" refer to?

A. Drawing property boundaries

B. Discriminatory lending practices

C. Marking properties for demolition

D. Highlighting important clauses in a contract

Answer: B

Redlining refers to discriminatory lending practices that deny loans or insurance to people based on their location, often targeting minority communities.

17. What is the difference between ethics and laws?

A. Ethics are legally binding, laws are not

B. Laws are legally binding, ethics are not

C. Ethics and laws are the same

D. Laws are optional, ethics are mandatory

Answer: B

Laws are legally binding rules that must be followed, while ethics are moral principles that guide behavior but are not legally enforceable.

18. What is the "doctrine of caveat emptor"?

   A. Let the buyer beware

   B. Let the seller beware

   C. Buyer's premium

   D. Seller's advantage

Answer: A

The doctrine of "caveat emptor" means "let the buyer beware," indicating that the buyer is responsible for due diligence.

19. What is a bilateral contract?

   A. A contract with only one party

   B. A contract with two parties

   C. A contract with multiple parties

   D. A contract that is not legally binding

Answer: B

A bilateral contract is a contract involving two parties where each party has made a promise to the other.

20. What is the role of a title company?

   A. To market properties

   B. To ensure the title is clear and prepare for its transfer

   C. To provide loans

   D. To build homes

Answer: B

The role of a title company is to ensure that the title to a piece of real estate is legitimate and to prepare for its transfer from the seller to the buyer.

21. What is the "dual agency" in real estate?

A. When an agent represents both the buyer and the seller
B. When two agents work for the same client
C. When an agent works for two different real estate firms
D. When an agent sells both commercial and residential properties

Answer: A

Dual agency occurs when a real estate agent represents both the buyer and the seller in the same transaction.

22. What does the Fair Housing Act prohibit?

A. Discrimination based on race, color, religion, sex, or national origin
B. All forms of discrimination
C. Discrimination based on financial status
D. Discrimination based on occupation

Answer: A

The Fair Housing Act prohibits discrimination in housing based on race, color, religion, sex, or national origin.

23. What is earnest money?

A. Money paid by the buyer at the time of the property closing
B. A refundable deposit
C. Money paid by the buyer to show serious intent to purchase
D. Money paid by the seller as a part of the listing agreement

Answer: C

Earnest money is money paid by the buyer to show serious intent to purchase the property.

24. What is a contingency in a real estate contract?

A. A binding clause
B. A non-negotiable term
C. A condition that must be met for the contract to be binding
D. A penalty for breach of contract

Answer: C

A contingency is a condition that must be met for the contract to be binding, such as a home inspection.

25. What is a fiduciary duty?

A. A legal obligation to act in the best interest of another
B. A duty to find the best property for a client
C. A duty to sell a property as quickly as possible
D. A duty to maximize profit

Answer: A

A fiduciary duty is a legal obligation to act in the best interest of another, such as a client.

26. What is a unilateral contract?

A. A contract where only one party makes a promise
B. A contract where both parties make promises
C. A contract that involves more than two parties
D. A contract that is not legally binding

Answer: A

A unilateral contract is a contract where only one party makes a promise, and the other has the option to complete the action.

➡ 27. What is the purpose of a disclosure statement?

A. To disclose the agent's commission
B. To disclose any known defects or issues with the property
C. To disclose the buyer's financial status
D. To disclose the terms of the mortgage

Answer: B

The purpose of a disclosure statement is to disclose any known defects or issues with the property to the buyer.

➡ 28. What does "time is of the essence" mean in a real estate contract?

A. Deadlines must be strictly adhered to
B. Time limits are flexible
C. The contract has no expiration date
D. The contract can be terminated at any time

Answer: A

"Time is of the essence" means that deadlines set forth in the contract must be strictly adhered to.

➡ 29. What is a quitclaim deed?

A. A deed that transfers property with no warranties
B. A deed that includes warranties
C. A deed that transfers leasehold interest
D. A deed that can be easily revoked

Answer: A

A quitclaim deed is a deed that transfers property with no warranties or guarantees.

30. What is the role of a notary public in a real estate transaction?

A. To negotiate the terms

B. To verify the identity of the parties and witness the signing of documents

C. To provide legal advice

D. To inspect the property

Answer: B

The role of a notary public is to verify the identity of the parties and witness the signing of important documents.

31. What is the primary purpose of a title search?

A. To determine the property's market value

B. To verify the legal owner of the property

C. To inspect the condition of the property

D. To assess property taxes

Answer: B

The primary purpose of a title search is to verify the legal owner of the property and ensure there are no liens or other encumbrances.

32. What is a "balloon payment" in a mortgage?

A. A small initial payment

B. A large final payment

C. A regular monthly payment

D. An extra payment to reduce interest

Answer: B

A balloon payment is a large final payment at the end of a loan term, usually after a series of smaller payments.

33. What is the "right of first refusal" in real estate?

A. The right to refuse a sale
B. The right to be the first to purchase a property before the owner sells it to another party
C. The right to refuse to pay rent
D. The right to refuse a home inspection

Answer: B

The right of first refusal allows an individual or entity the opportunity to purchase a property before the owner sells it to another party.

34. What is a "listing agreement"?

A. An agreement between buyer and seller
B. An agreement between a seller and a real estate agent
C. An agreement between a buyer and a real estate agent
D. An agreement between two real estate agents

Answer: B

A listing agreement is a contract between a seller and a real estate agent outlining the terms under which the agent will sell the property.

35. What does "under contract" mean in real estate?

A. The property is being appraised
B. The property is being inspected
C. An offer on the property has been accepted, but the sale is not yet complete
D. The property has been sold

Answer: C

"Under contract" means that an offer on the property has been accepted, but the sale is not yet complete, pending contingencies or other terms.

➭36. What is the role of a fiduciary in a real estate transaction?

A. To act in the best interest of the client

B. To maximize profits for the brokerage

C. To represent both buyer and seller equally

D. To ensure the property passes inspection

Answer: A

The role of a fiduciary is to act in the best interest of the client, whether that's the buyer or the seller.

➭37. What does "escrow" refer to in real estate?

A. A type of mortgage loan

B. A neutral third party holding funds or documents until conditions are met

C. A binding contract between buyer and seller

D. A home inspection report

Answer: B

Escrow refers to a neutral third party holding funds or documents until certain conditions are met in a real estate transaction.

➭38. What is a "contingency" in a real estate contract?

A. A penalty for late payment

B. A condition that must be met for the contract to proceed

C. An optional add-on to the property

D. A mandatory fee paid to the real estate agent

Answer: B

A contingency is a condition that must be met for the contract to proceed, such as a successful home inspection.

39. What does "amortization" mean in the context of a mortgage?

A. The process of increasing the loan amount
B. The process of paying off the loan over time
C. The process of adjusting the interest rate
D. The process of transferring the loan to another lender

Answer: B

Amortization is the process of paying off a loan over time through regular payments.

40. What is "due diligence" in real estate?

A. The responsibility to investigate a property before purchase
B. The obligation to pay property taxes
C. The requirement to obtain a mortgage pre-approval
D. The duty to disclose all known defects to a buyer

Answer: A

Due diligence is the responsibility of the buyer to investigate a property thoroughly before completing the purchase.

41. What is "redlining" in the context of real estate?

A. Drawing property boundaries
B. Discriminatory practice affecting mortgage availability

C. A type of home inspection

D. A negotiation strategy

Answer: B

Redlining is a discriminatory practice where mortgage lenders deny loans or insurance to certain areas based on racial or ethnic composition.

42. What does "title insurance" protect against?

A. Property damage

B. Mortgage default

C. Legal claims against property ownership

D. Loss of rental income

Answer: C

Title insurance protects against legal claims challenging the ownership of the property.

43. What is "dual agency" in real estate?

A. When an agent represents both the buyer and the seller

B. When two agents from the same brokerage represent the buyer and the seller

C. When an agent represents two buyers for the same property

D. When an agent represents two sellers for different properties

Answer: A

Dual agency occurs when a real estate agent represents both the buyer and the seller in the same transaction. This can create a conflict of interest and is illegal in some states.

44. What is a "balloon mortgage"?

A. A mortgage with fluctuating interest rates

B. A mortgage that requires a large final payment

C. A mortgage with no down payment

D. A mortgage paid off in less than 5 years

Answer: B

A balloon mortgage requires a large final payment at the end of the loan term.

45. What is "blockbusting"?

A. Building multiple properties in a short time

B. Encouraging people to sell their homes by instigating fear of a changing neighborhood

C. The process of rezoning land

D. Buying large blocks of property for development

Answer: B

Blockbusting is the practice of encouraging people to sell their homes by instigating fear, often related to racial, ethnic, or social change in a neighborhood.

46. What is a "1031 exchange"?

A. A tax-deferred property exchange

B. A type of mortgage loan

C. A property auction

D. An open house event

Answer: A

A 1031 exchange allows the owner to sell a property and reinvest the proceeds in a new property while deferring capital gains tax.

47. What is "eminent domain"?

A. The right of the government to acquire private property for public use

B. The highest legal ownership of property

C. A type of zoning regulation

D. A clause in a mortgage contract

Answer: A

Eminent domain is the right of the government to acquire private property for public use, usually with compensation.

48. What is "equity" in real estate?

A. The market value of a property

B. The difference between the property's market value and the remaining mortgage balance

C. The initial down payment

D. The annual property tax

Answer: B

Equity is the difference between the market value of the property and the remaining balance on any loans secured by the property.

49. What is "escrow" in a real estate transaction?

A. A legal arrangement where a third party holds funds or documents

B. The initial offer made by a buyer

C. The final stage of mortgage approval

D. A type of home inspection

Answer: A

Escrow is a legal arrangement in which a third party temporarily holds funds or documents until the conditions of a contract are met.

50. What is "net operating income" in real estate investment?

A. Gross income minus operating expenses

B. Gross income plus operating expenses

C. Mortgage payments minus rental income

D. Property value minus mortgage balance

Answer: A

Net operating income is the gross income generated by a property minus the operating expenses, not including mortgage payments or taxes.

Day of the Exam

The day of the real estate exam is a culmination of all the hard work, study sessions, and practice exams you've undertaken. It's natural to feel a mix of excitement and anxiety, but preparation is key to calming those nerves and performing well. This chapter aims to guide you through the day of the exam, from the moment you wake up to the moment you complete the test.

- Morning Routine

Wake Up Early

It's crucial to wake up early to give yourself ample time to prepare mentally and physically. A rushed morning can lead to unnecessary stress.

Breakfast

Eat a balanced breakfast that includes protein, fruits, and whole grains. Avoid sugary cereals or pastries that can lead to a sugar crash later.

Dress Comfortably

Wear comfortable clothing that adheres to the exam center's dress code. Layering is a good idea as it allows you to adjust to the room's temperature.

Gather Essentials

Make sure you have all the necessary identification, admission tickets, and any allowed materials like a basic calculator. Double-check these items against the list provided by the exam center.

- Travel to the Exam Center

Leave Early

Account for traffic, parking, and any last-minute issues. Aim to arrive at least 30 minutes before the exam starts.

Public Transport

If you're using public transport, know the schedule and stops. Always have a backup plan.

Parking

If you're driving, know where you can park and how much time it will take to walk from the parking area to the exam center.

- At the Exam Center

Check-in Process

Upon arrival, you'll likely go through a check-in process that includes ID verification and storing your belongings in a locker.

The Waiting Area

Use this time to relax and do some light review if you wish. Avoid cramming as it can increase stress levels.

Restroom Break

Take a restroom break before entering the exam room, even if you don't feel like you need to. It's better to be comfortable during the exam.

- During the Exam

Time Management

Keep an eye on the clock. It's easy to lose track of time when you're focused.

Read Carefully

Read each question and all the answer choices carefully. Misreading a question can lead to a wrong answer.

Mark and Move

If you're unsure about a question, mark it and move on. Return to it later if time permits.

Stay Calm

If you start to feel anxious, take deep breaths to calm your nerves. Remember, you've prepared for this.

- After the Exam

Review

Some exams allow for a brief review period. Use this time wisely to revisit questions you were unsure about.

Submission

Once you're done, submit your exam and leave the room quietly, respecting those who are still working.

Collect Belongings

Don't forget to collect any belongings from the locker or storage area.

- Conclusion

The day of the exam can be stressful, but adequate preparation can make it manageable. Follow these guidelines to ensure you're as ready as you can be, both mentally and logistically, to tackle the exam successfully.

After the Exam: Next Steps

Congratulations on completing your real estate exam! The journey doesn't end here, though. This chapter will guide you through the steps you should take after the exam, from understanding your results to planning your career in real estate.

- Understanding Your Results

Immediate Results

Some testing centers provide immediate results, while others may take a few days or weeks. Know the procedure for your specific exam.

Score Breakdown

Understanding the breakdown of your score can provide insights into your strengths and weaknesses. This is particularly useful if you need to retake the exam.

Pass or Fail

If you pass, you'll usually receive a certificate or license number. If you fail, don't be discouraged. Review your weak areas and retake the exam.

- What To Do If You Pass

Celebrate

Take some time to celebrate your hard work and achievement. You've earned it!

Licensing

Submit any additional documents to your state's real estate commission to finalize your license.

Join a Brokerage

Most states require new agents to work under a broker for a certain period. Research brokerages to find one that aligns with your career goals.

Continuous Learning

The real estate industry is ever-changing. Keep up with laws, market trends, and other educational opportunities.

- What To Do If You Fail

Review the Exam

Go through the score breakdown and identify the areas where you struggled.

Create a Study Plan

Based on your weaknesses, create a new study plan. Consider hiring a tutor or taking additional courses.

Retake the Exam

Most states allow you to retake the exam after a certain period. Use this time wisely to prepare.

- Career Planning

Set Goals

Whether you're new to real estate or a seasoned professional, setting career goals can guide your actions and decisions.

Networking

Build a strong network with other real estate professionals. Attend industry events, join real estate associations, and don't underestimate the power of social media.

Marketing Yourself

Create a professional website, print business cards, and use social media to market yourself. Consider specialized areas like commercial real estate or property management as career options.

Legal Obligations and Ethics

Continuing Education

Many states require ongoing education to renew your license. Stay updated on this as failing to meet the requirements can result in your license being revoked.

Ethical Practices

Maintain high ethical standards in all your transactions. Unethical behavior can lead to legal issues and damage your reputation.

- Financial Planning

Taxes

As a real estate agent, you're generally considered a self-employed individual for tax purposes. Keep track of your expenses and income, and consider hiring an accountant familiar with real estate.

Retirement

It's never too early to think about retirement. Look into retirement plans suitable for self-employed individuals.

- Conclusion

The period after the real estate exam is crucial for setting the stage for your career. Whether you pass or fail, there are clear steps you can take to move forward. From understanding your exam results to career planning and beyond, this chapter aims to provide a comprehensive guide for life after the real estate exam.

Career Development

Congratulations on passing your real estate exam and obtaining your license! Now comes the exciting part—building a successful career. This chapter will guide you through the various stages of career development in real estate, from choosing a specialty to scaling your business.

- Choosing a Specialty

Residential Real Estate

This is the most common starting point for many agents. You'll be helping individuals and families buy, sell, or rent homes.

Commercial Real Estate

This involves working with businesses to buy, sell, or lease office spaces, retail locations, and other commercial properties.

Property Management

Here, you'll manage properties on behalf of owners, ensuring they are well-maintained, occupied, and profitable.

Luxury Real Estate

This niche focuses on high-end properties and typically requires a strong network and a deep understanding of the luxury market.

- Joining a Brokerage

Independent vs. Franchise

Independent brokerages offer more freedom but less support. Franchises provide robust training programs but may require fees.

Commission Split

Understand the commission structure. Some brokerages offer a higher split but fewer services, while others may offer a lower split but more support.

Culture and Environment

The brokerage's culture can significantly impact your job satisfaction and success. Choose a brokerage that aligns with your values and career goals.

- Building Your Brand

Personal Website

A professional website can serve as a portfolio showcasing your expertise, listings, and client testimonials.

Social Media

Platforms like Instagram, LinkedIn, and Facebook are excellent for networking and reaching a broader audience.

Business Cards and Flyers

Invest in high-quality business cards and flyers for offline marketing.

- Networking

Real Estate Associations

Join local or national real estate associations to stay updated on industry trends and network with professionals.

Community Involvement

Participate in community events to build your local presence.

Mentorship

Consider finding a mentor who can guide you through the complexities of the real estate business.

- Skill Development

Negotiation Skills

Being a skilled negotiator can make a significant difference in your transactions.

Legal Knowledge

Understanding contracts, disclosures, and real estate laws is crucial.

Market Analysis

Being able to analyze market trends will make you an invaluable resource to your clients.

- Scaling Your Business

Hiring an Assistant

As your business grows, administrative tasks can become overwhelming. Hiring an assistant can free up time for revenue-generating activities.

Forming a Team

A team can help you handle more clients and listings, but it also comes with the challenge of management.

Technology

Invest in real estate software for customer relationship management (CRM), market analysis, and virtual tours.

- Continuing Education

License Renewal

Most states require periodic license renewal, which may involve continuing education.

Special Certifications

Earning additional certifications can make you more marketable.

- Financial Planning

Savings and Investments

Set aside a portion of your earnings for savings and investments.

Retirement Planning

Consider long-term financial stability by investing in retirement plans tailored for self-employed individuals.

- Conclusion

Career development in real estate is a continuous journey. From the moment you decide to enter the field, each step you take contributes to your professional growth. This chapter has aimed to provide a roadmap for that journey, offering insights and tips that can help you navigate the complexities of the real estate industry successfully.

Conclusion

Dear Aspiring Real Estate Professional,

As you reach the final chapter of "Pennsylvania Real Estate License Exam: Best Test Prep Book to Help You Get Your License!", you've already taken a monumental step towards a fulfilling career in real estate. This book was designed to be more than just a study guide; it's a comprehensive roadmap to success in the Pennsylvania real estate industry.

The Scope of This Book

From the moment you opened the first page, we embarked on a comprehensive journey together. We delved into the nuances of the Pennsylvania real estate market, dissected the eligibility criteria, and walked you through the application process. We explored the exam format in detail and discussed various specialty areas within real estate. We even covered what to expect on the day of the exam and the steps to take afterward. Each chapter was meticulously crafted to provide you with the most current and relevant information to not only pass your exam but also to thrive in your subsequent career.

The Value of Mock Exams

The mock exams and practice questions included in this book were not just an afterthought. They were carefully designed to mimic the actual exam you will face. The aim was to provide you with a realistic testing experience to better prepare you for the real thing. The questions spanned the range of topics covered in the book, challenging you to apply what you've learned in a practical context.

The Ever-Evolving Real Estate Landscape

While this book aims to be a comprehensive resource, the world of real estate is dynamic and ever-changing. Laws are updated, market conditions fluctuate, and new technologies are continually emerging. As you move forward in your career, it's crucial to stay updated and adapt to these changes. Continuous learning is not just a buzzword; it's a necessity for anyone looking to have a long, successful career in real estate.

Ethics and Professionalism

One of the most critical aspects we covered is the importance of ethics and legal considerations in real estate. As a real estate professional, you'll be entrusted with significant responsibilities. Upholding ethical standards isn't just about adhering to laws; it's about building trust and credibility in the market. Your reputation is your most valuable asset, and this book aims to equip you with the moral compass needed to navigate complex ethical dilemmas you may encounter.

Looking Ahead: Your Career Development

Passing the exam is a significant achievement, but it's just the beginning. The chapters on career development were included to help you think long-term. Whether you're interested in residential, commercial, or industrial real estate, there are numerous paths you can take to specialize and advance your career.

Final Words

As you close this book, remember that the end of this guide is the beginning of your real-world journey. The knowledge and skills you've acquired are tools you'll use every day in your new career. We wish you all the best in your exam and your future endeavors in the Pennsylvania real estate industry.

Thank you for allowing us to be part of your educational journey. Here's to your success!

Made in United States
North Haven, CT
12 February 2024

48607396R00139